BETWEEN
THE
TIMES

BETWEEN THE TIMES

MALACHI : THE LAST PROPHET

BEFORE CENTURIES OF SILENCE

R. T. Kendall

CHRISTIAN FOCUS

For
Dr Anita Davies and Dr Naomal and Joyce Soysa

© R. T. Kendall

ISBN 1 85792 792 3

Published in 2003
by
Christian Focus Publications Ltd,
Geanies House, Fearn,
Ross-shire, IV20 ITW,
Great Britain

www.christianfocus.com

Cover design by Alister MacInnes

Printed and bound by
Cox & Wyman, Reading, Berkshire

CONTENTS

Preface.. 7

1. The Sovereignty of God................................. 9

2. Afraid you aren't loved? 15

3. Honouring God 23

4. Begging God - Would you do it? 29

5. Cheap Grace 35

6. Taking God for Granted 41

7. When the Church does more Harm than Good   45

8. Should a Christian marry a non-Christian? 51

9. When Tears don't Help................................ 57

10. When God rolls up his sleeves...................... 63

11. Marriage, Infidelity and divorce.................... 71

12. When believers question God 79

13. Prayer suddenly Answered 87

14. Do we want Revival after all?....................... 95

15. Judgment in God's House 101

16. The Unchanging God 109

17. Coming Home... 117

18. Is it the Principle or is it the Money? 123

19. Can we prove God? 129

20. Unlocking the Gates of Heaven 135

21. Does God have Feelings? 141

22. The Eavesdropping God 147

23. God's Book of Remembrance 151

24. How God shows his Love 155

25. God's Class System 161

26. When Evil is no More 167

27. The Fire of God 173

28. Just Healing 179

29. The Sun of Righteousness 183

30. Just Free 187

31. Why Remember God's law? 193

32. The Last Word................................... 197

PREFACE

I am so honoured that Christian Focus Publications would invite me to do another book with them and I want to thank William Mackenzie for his continued confidence in my ministry. I do not have words to express how much I appreciate having a reformed publisher who believes in me and enables me to have a continuing ministry after my retirement. This book is based on sermons that I preached near the end of my ministry in Westminster Chapel in London. It is, in fact, the first book of my sermons that has been published since my retirement in February 2002, at which time we moved to the Florida Keys.

This book is lovingly dedicated to Dr Anita Davies and Dr Naomal and Joyce Soysa who have been special friends over the years we were at Westminster Chapel. Dr Davies, who was homeopathic physician to the late Queen Elizabeth, the Queen Mother, looked after Louise and me with utmost faithfulness. Dr Soysa, a deacon at Westminster Chapel, has equally taken care of us. We were blessed to have people like them, especially in our times of need. Not every minister has a doctor in his church, but I had both of them, and I thank God for them.

I warmly thank Irene Howat for the hard work and care she has put into the editing these sermons.

May God make this book a blessing to you.

R. T. Kendall

Key Largo, Florida
July, 2003

1

THE SOVEREIGNTY OF GOD

'I have loved you,' says the LORD. 'But you ask, 'How have you loved us?' 'Was not Esau Jacob's brother?' the LORD says. 'Yet I have loved Jacob, but Esau I have hated, and I have turned his mountains into a wasteland and left his inheritance to the desert jackals.' Edom may say, 'Though we have been crushed, we will rebuild the ruins.' But this is what the LORD Almighty says: 'They may build, but I will demolish. They will be called The Wicked Land, a people always under the wrath of the LORD. You will see it with your own eyes and say, 'Great is the LORD – even beyond the borders of Israel!' (Malachi 1:2-5).

The Book of Malachi, the last of the Old Testament, was probably written at around 450 BC. The theme of the book is *You are Loved* and its opening words are: *'An oracle: The word of the LORD to Israel through Malachi. "I have loved you," says the LORD' (1:1).* How does it make you feel to know that someone loves you? Many people are just a little uneasy when someone comes up to them and says, 'I love you.' Sometimes I say it to people I know really well. Just as I go off the telephone I say, 'Love you,' and they don't know how to respond. 'Right, oh well, um, um,' is often all I get in return. Once in a while, if they are used to me telling them I love them, they say, 'Oh well, same to you.' But it is a good feeling to know that you are loved. I want to hear it from my wife every day, and I guess she wants to hear it from me every day too. Victor Hugo, the nineteenth-century French writer, said, 'The supreme happiness in life is the conviction that we are loved.' Michael Eaton, a missionary in Nairobi, once told me that he saw a sticker in a car window that said, 'Someone in Kenya loves me'!

We all have a need to be loved. When people are difficult to understand, when I wonder what makes them tick, I find that what they most need, and what they most want, is to be loved. There is nothing that breaks the hardest heart like the feeling of being loved. All of us can face terrible opposition and suffering if we feel approved of, accepted and loved by someone whose opinion matters to us. There may be people out there who care about your approval and perhaps you have never told them that you love them. Some readers ought to get on the phone today to their parents, while they are still alive, and say, 'I love you.' I remember how angry I used to be with my dad when a letter arrived from him saying, 'Dear Son, I wrote you on the eighteenth, you would have got our letter on the twenty-second, but I notice you didn't write until the twenty-fifth.' Then the letters stopped coming. Dad had Alzheimers. I could tell him now that I love him, but it would mean nothing at all. My dear Dad is now in heaven.

Let me tell you about Uncle Buddy Robinson. He was illiterate, having quit school at the age of nine. And he was tongue-tied. If ever there was somebody who had no future it was Buddy Robinson. A preacher who got to know him told the man, 'Bud, I love you.' Robinson looked up and said, 'What?' 'I love you,' the preacher repeated. 'Nobody has ever said that to me before,' gasped Buddy. The preacher smiled. 'Will you come to church with me tonight?' he asked. 'Don't know what it is or where it is,' Buddy replied, 'but I'll go.' He sat through the sermon, at the end of which there was an altar call. 'Bud, will you go to the altar?' the preacher asked. 'Don't know what it is or where it is, but I'll go,' Bud said, 'for you told me you loved me.' He was converted soon afterwards, and he became an evangelist in the Church of the Nazarene in which I was brought up. It is estimated that Bud led over a quarter of a million people to Christ, and it all began because he was told that he was loved.

There is an even greater feeling than knowing another person loves you, and that is knowing that God loves you. There is no greater feeling than that; there is nothing like it. When I feel that God loves me and approves of me I can face a thousand foes. And the message of Malachi is just that, *You are loved.* *'"I have loved you," says the Lord'* (1:2). We all have skeletons in our cupboards, and God knows every one of them, yet he still says, 'I love you.'

Martin Luther called John 3:16 the Bible in a nutshell, and that's what it is. *'For God so loved the world that he gave his one and only Son, that whoever believes in him shall not perish but have eternal life.'*

But knowing that you are loved isn't the end of the story. Malachi goes on to say: *'But you ask, "How have you loved us?"'* *"Was not Esau Jacob's brother?" the LORD says. "Yet I have loved Jacob, but Esau I have hated, and I have turned his mountains into a wasteland and left his inheritance to the desert jackals"'* (1:2-3).

That use of 'love' and 'hate' is a common Hebraic idiom in which they are not to be taken absolutely but by comparison. When they are together, as they are in this verse, love means preferred and hate means loved less. Which brings us to the subject of this chapter, the sovereignty of God. I like the phrase *'I have loved Jacob'*, I am not so happy with *'Esau I have hated'*. I wish that were not there. Whether we like it or not, the verse shows that God chooses some but not all. Charles Spurgeon used to offend his fellow Calvinists when he prayed publicly, 'Lord, send in all thine elect, then elect some more.' Spurgeon believed in the absolute sovereignty of God, his right to do what he pleases at any time with anyone. When he was preaching to some ministers on the importance of soul-winning, Spurgeon said they should try to convert everybody as though they were all God's elect. Afterwards someone asked him, 'But, Mr Spurgeon, what if we convert one of the non-elect?' Spurgeon patted the man on the back and said, 'Well, God will forgive you for that.'

Although we read here, *'I have loved Jacob, but Esau I have hated,'* we read in Hebrews 12:15: *'See to it that no-one misses the grace of God and that no bitter root grows up to cause trouble and defile many. See that no-one is sexually immoral, or is godless like Esau, who for a single meal sold his inheritance rights as the oldest son. Afterwards, as you know, when he wanted to inherit this blessing, he was rejected. He could bring about no change of mind, though he sought the blessing with tears.'*

Jacob could take no credit because God loved him. Esau could not blame God because he chose to live in the here and now, voluntarily giving up his birthright. What he did, he did by deliberate choice. Salvation is all of God's choice. No Christian can boast of his faith and say, 'Look what I have done!' In the sovereignty of God salvation is his to give or to withhold. Some people don't like it that God has that right, but he is God and he does whatever he wants.

Sometimes we do not want God to be God, we want God to be like us. We want God to jump if we just look up to him; we want God to salute us and do our bidding. But instead, he said to Moses, *'I will have mercy on whom I will have mercy, and I will have compassion on whom I will have compassion'* (Ex. 33:19). That is God's right.

God sometimes chooses to withhold his mercy. He says, *'"Esau I have hated, and I have turned his mountains into a wasteland and left his inheritance to the desert jackals." Edom may say, "Though we have been crushed, we will rebuild the ruins." But this is what the LORD Almighty says: "They may build, but I will demolish. ... the wrath of the LORD ... You will see it with your own eyes"'* (1:4-5). That is enough to bring us to our knees.

The only way to be saved is to ask God for mercy. Mercy, to be mercy, can be given or withheld and justice be done in either case. Jesus described two people in prayer. '*Two men went up to the temple to pray, one a Pharisee and the other a tax collector. The Pharisee stood up and prayed about himself: "God, I thank you that I am not like other men ... or even like this tax collector" ... But the tax collector stood at a distance. He would not even look up to heaven, but beat his breast and said, "God, have mercy on me, a sinner." I tell you that this man, rather than the other, went home justified before God. For everyone who exalts himself will be humbled, and he who humbles himself will be exalted*' (Luke 18:10-14).

If you want to compare yourself with others, God says you are lost. You should climb down from your pride and say, 'God be merciful to me a sinner. I'd be so grateful.' Because God decides to whom to show mercy, it makes all the difference in the world how we approach him. He is sovereign. When you know that he has said, '*I will have mercy on whom I will have mercy, and I will have compassion on whom I will have compassion*' (*Ex.* 33:19), you come to your knees and say, 'Will you be gracious to me?'

This word at the beginning of the Book of Malachi was an oracle to the people of Israel. You say, 'Well that is fine, God loved Israel, but I am a Gentile.' But in Romans 9:6, Paul says, '*It is not as though God's word had failed. For not all who are descended from Israel are Israel.*' God has widened the family. His family was not to be continued along racial lines, but through those who would hear the gospel and respond to it. There is one requirement for being loved. We find it at the end of the book of Revelation. '*The Spirit and the bride say, "Come!" And let him who hears say, "Come." Whoever is thirsty, let him come; and whoever wishes, let him take the free gift of the water of life*' (22:17).

The requirement for being loved is to know we are in need of his love, and the requirement for being satisfied is that we are thirsty.

2

AFRAID YOU AREN'T LOVED?

'I have loved you,' says the LORD. 'But you ask, 'How have you loved us?' 'Was not Esau Jacob's brother?' the LORD says. 'Yet I have loved Jacob, but Esau I have hated, and I have turned his mountains into a wasteland and left his inheritance to the desert jackals.' Edom may say, 'Though we have been crushed, we will rebuild the ruins,' But this is what the LORD Almighty says: 'They may build, but I will demolish. They will be called The Wicked Land, a people always under the wrath of the LORD. You will see it with your own eyes and say, 'Great is the LORD – even beyond the borders of Israel!' (Malachi 1:2-5).

Malachi begins his book by telling the people of Israel that they are loved, and he continues it by telling them that they are still loved. Sometimes we need reassurance because, although we've heard that we are loved, after a while we think maybe we have said something we shouldn't have said, or done something we shouldn't have done, and we are not loved any longer. The people of Israel to whom this prophecy was directed knew that Jacob was loved. But that was then, hundreds of years ago. Malachi's message was that Jacob was loved then, and you are Jacob, you are Israel, and nothing has changed. You are still loved now. They asked God, *'How have you loved us?'* Were they asking if it were possible that God could still love them? Some people would give anything in the world to find out for themselves again that they really are loved by the one who matters, God himself.

The word Malachi means 'messenger' and there is some doubt whether the writer just used the word Malachi or if that was what his name actually was. His prophecy, his message, turned out to be the last book of the Old Testament. It was about 500 years before another inspired book of Scripture was written. Therefore the last word that Israel had from God before the coming of Christ was, '*You are loved.*' Often when Louise and I are on the phone to each other the last thing we say is, 'Love you.' Some time ago, when I went on a plane journey, our son TR wrote me a note, 'Love you, TR.' I kept it with me and read it on the plane. It made me feel good. Malachi's message from God was the same as TR's message to me. 'I love you.'

The people to whom Malachi spoke were very discouraged. Israel had been in Babylon in captivity, and much had happened since they returned home to make their spirits low. Although the temple had been rebuilt, and the people had had a new beginning, somehow or other they did not feel restored. For one thing, the royal line of David had not been restored. There was not a Judean king; they were actually under the rule of the Persian governor. The people were living in their own land, but it didn't seem right. And the temple, though rebuilt, was so small compared to Solomon's temple that it bore no resemblance to its magnificent predecessor. Not only that, the fact that there were people living in Judea who weren't Jewish, and who had no interest in Israel's historic faith, meant that there were in effect two kinds of Jews.

There would seem to be two kinds of Christians today, those who have a saving faith in Jesus and those who come into the church for aesthetic and historical reasons, believing that is what Christianity is all about. They are proud of their heritage; they want churches and cathedrals preserved just as they are. Such people may be very strong on the Book of Common Prayer, and on a whole list of religious ceremonies, but the truth is that they are not excited about the faith. It is possible to be in the church and not be converted. I can't think of anything worse than to be part of the visible body of Christ, and to think you are saved, when in fact you are lost. And it was just the same in Malachi's day. Those who really were part of the historic faith were opposed and persecuted by those who were not. Malachi addresses himself to the persecuted, and he tells them, 'God loves you.' They felt that the good old days were gone forever; there didn't even seem to be any real justice. Malachi addressed people who felt unloved, down and depressed.

When you don't feel loved it is hard to be convinced that you are loved, even though you want to feel loved more than anything else in the world. Some feel unloved because it doesn't seem fair that God permits evil and suffering in the world. They say, 'Look at me in my condition. Look at all that I have been through. Why is it that good things happen to bad people and bad things happen to good people? Why the suffering? Why the hardship? Life isn't fair. I haven't done anything to deserve this. How can I feel that God loves me?'

Others feel unloved because they've been rejected in the past, sometimes by their own parents. It is hard for me to identify with anybody who says that they weren't loved by their parents because I was doted on by my father and mother. But those who have felt rejected by their parents have a problem: often it is hard for them to believe it when they are told that their heavenly Father loves them. They were so used to criticism that they find it hard to be accepted. 'My parents don't love me,' they say, 'so why should I think that God does?'

There are others, backsliders who have wandered away from God, who find his acceptance hard to take. They have slipped back from what they used to be. These people may have started well, but they feel they have let God down. There are some, of course, who feel like that but who are not converted, because it is possible to become a member of the church by making a nominal profession of faith, having been pushed into it by peer pressure or for some other such reason. This word from Malachi is not specially for them; they need to be converted.

Some years ago a person came into the vestry and I said, 'Are you saved?' 'No, No, no way could I be saved,' he replied. 'I have wandered from God and I am living in an awful situation. No, I can't possibly be saved.' I said, 'If you stood before God and he were to ask you why he should let you into heaven, what would you say?' 'Well,' he replied, 'the only way God could let me in is because Jesus died for me on the cross.' 'You couldn't have said that if there were not life in you even as I speak,' I told him. And that was the most thrilling thing that man could hear. He was expecting me to come down hard on him, demanding how he dared to let God down. 'Are you saying that I am still saved?' he asked. I told him that was exactly what I was saying. That changed his life. It made him want to come back to God.

The good news is that we are loved with an everlasting love. God is married to the Christian, even the backslider. Listen to these words from the apostle Paul. '*If God is for us, who can be against us? ... Who will bring any charge against those whom God has chosen? It is God who justifies. Who is he that condemns? Christ Jesus, who died – more than that, who was raised to life – is at the right hand of God and is also interceding for us. Who shall separate us from the love of Christ? Shall trouble or hardship or persecution or famine or nakedness or danger or sword? As it is written: "For your sake we face death all day long; we are considered as sheep to be slaughtered." No, in all these things we are more than conquerors through him who loved us. For I am convinced that neither death nor life, neither angels nor demons, neither the present nor the future, nor any powers, neither height nor depth, nor anything else in all creation, will be able to separate us from the love of God that is in Christ Jesus our Lord*' (Rom. 8:31-39).

Perhaps you don't feel loved because there has been no answer to prayer lately, and you are beginning to think there is something wrong with you, or that you have done something to offend God. If that's the case, remember that sometimes God takes a long time answering prayer. I don't know why that is, I only know that any prayer prayed in the will of God will be answered, because we are told that if we ask anything according to his will he hears and answers. *'This is the confidence we have in approaching God: that if we ask anything according to his will, he hears us ... – whatever we ask – we know that we have what we asked of him'* (I John 5:14-15). A lot of people give up waiting. But God's slowness to answer may be a test of our faith.

Perhaps your sins are so grievous you've concluded that God cannot possibly love you, that there is no forgiveness for what you have done. The Bible tells us that there is an unpardonable sin. Matthew and Mark say that if we blaspheme the Holy Spirit there is no forgiveness in this world, or in the world to come. The blaspheming of the Spirit is the denial of the Spirit's testimony that God came in the flesh. Any spirit that will not confess that God came in the flesh is antichrist; such a person is not saved. But anybody who can say that Jesus Christ is the Son of God – God as though he were not man, man as though he were not God – has not committed the unpardonable sin.

It may be that you accept in your head that God loves you but you don't feel it in your heart. If that is the case you are like those to whom Malachi was sent, and he knew that he had his work cut out to persuade them. The people were being chastened. They were in the line of Jacob, who was loved, not in the line of nominal Jews who had no interest in the historic faith of Israel. Hebrews 12:6 says, *'The Lord disciplines those he loves, and he punishes everyone he accepts as a son.'*

The word chasten, or discipline, comes from a Greek word that means enforced learning. It is used when God teaches us a lesson and we learn it despite ourselves. You may not feel that you want to be loved by being chastened; you don't want God to teach you lessons by forcing them on you. But the essence of

19

his chastening is hiding his face, and it was no different in the lives of the Israelites. These people were wrong to think that God was not dealing with their enemy. They were wrong to say that nothing good was happening to them and everything good was happening to their enemy.

'You are wrong,' says Malachi, I have loved (preferred) Jacob, but Esau I have hated (loved less). Martin Luther said that he expected to see Esau in heaven; that this was not referring to Esau not being loved by God, and that it is not saying that he could not be saved. The point is that Israel had a special love. As for Esau, *'The LORD says ... "I have turned his mountains into a wasteland and left his inheritance to the desert jackals." Edom may say, "Though we have been crushed, we will rebuild the ruins." But this is what the LORD Almighty says: "They may build, but I will demolish"'* (1:3-4).

Look what is happening to Edom, Malachi is saying, God is dealing with Edom because he prefers Israel. It has always been a problem for Christians that good things happen to those who are wicked, while we are serving the Lord and nothing good seems to happen to us. In Psalm 73 the psalmist says, *'I envied the arrogant when I saw the prosperity of the wicked. They have no struggles; their bodies are healthy and strong. They are free from the burdens common to man; they are not plagued by human ills'* (vs. 3-5). The psalmist feels that he has been plagued all day long. He goes on. *'Surely in vain have I kept my heart pure; in vain have I washed my hands in innocence'* (v.13).

Perhaps you feel like that. You have resisted temptation. You had an opportunity to make money and you knew it wouldn't be right. You had an opportunity to sleep with a boyfriend or girlfriend and you didn't take it. Now you are saying, 'Surely I have kept my heart pure in vain.' The psalm continues, *'When I tried to understand all this, it was oppressive to me till I entered the sanctuary of God; then I understood their final destiny'* (vs.

16-17). Then he realized, *'Surely you place them on slippery ground; you cast them down to ruin'* (v.18).

Malachi comes along and his opening words are, this is *'an oracle'*. In fact, he says it is a word from the Lord. There was an expression that prophets used: 'the burden of the Lord.' They used it when God put something in their heart. God put this message in Malachi's heart and he faithfully discharged it. Do we do that? I heard of a Christian who was hitchhiking when a very nice car drove up and the driver offered him a lift. As they drove along the road God gave the Christian a burden for the man who was driving. He knew he had to witness to him. 'Excuse me, sir,' he said, 'for some reason I have to talk to you. I am a Christian, but do you know that you are saved?' He shared the gospel and, as he continued to talk, the driver began to weep. They pulled over to the side of the road and the man received Jesus Christ as his Saviour. That Christian was faithful to the burden God gave him.

Five years later, the hitchhiker wondered what had become of the man he led to the Lord. He knew the driver was from Chicago and, as he was going there, he decided to find him. When he found the driver's place of business he was told he could not speak to the man but he could speak to his wife. He did that, and as he explained why he was looking for her husband, the woman began to weep. She asked if he knew the date that meeting had taken place. When he gave her the date, the woman couldn't believe her ears. She said, 'I have been a Christian for years and I prayed for my husband to be saved. On that date, and it must have been just minutes after you talked to him, he had a head-on collision and was killed. I didn't know until now that he was saved.' When you have a burden don't ignore it; it may be a matter of life and death.

Malachi's oracle, *'I have loved you'*, was not meant just for those who heard him speak, it is for us too. God's Word tells us that while we were yet sinners Christ died for us, that we are not

21

saved by our works but by Christ. If we were saved by our works then nobody would be saved, because the standard of entrance into heaven is so high that no-one ever comes up to it. Why God loves as he does is beyond explanation. God's love for us in Christ is his last word on the subject, just as God's last word to his people was that they were loved. About 500 years later, through the house of David, God's Messiah came to Israel.

3

HONOURING GOD

'A son honours his father, and a servant his master. If I am a father, where is the honour due to me? If I am a master, where is the respect due to me?' says the LORD Almighty. 'It is you, O priests, who show contempt for my name. But you ask, "How have we shown contempt for your name?" 'You place defiled food on my altar.' But you ask, "How have we defiled you?" By saying that the LORD's table is contemptible. When you bring blind animals for sacrifice, is that not wrong? When you sacrifice crippled or diseased animals, is that not wrong? Try offering them to your governor! Would he be pleased with you? Would he accept you?' says the LORD Almighty. 'Now implore God to be gracious to us. With such offerings from your hands, will he accept you?' – says the LORD Almighty (Malachi 1:6-9).

The Israelites had been dishonouring God by offering substandard sacrifices. God had plenty to say about that through Malachi. The Lord had given clear instructions regarding sacrifices, *'The animals you choose must be year-old males without defect, and you may take them from the sheep or the goats'* (Ex. 12:5). *'If the offering is a burnt offering from the herd, he is to offer a male without defect'* ... *If the offering is a burnt offering from the flock, from either the sheep or the goats, he is to offer a male without defect'* (Lev. 1:3,10). *'Do not offer to the LORD the blind, the injured or the maimed, or anything with warts or festering or running sores'* (Lev. 22:22). *'If an animal has a defect, is lame or blind, or has any serious flaw, you must not sacrifice it to the LORD your God'* (Deut. 15:21).

Things had degenerated to such a state in Israel by Malachi's time that they were actually bringing crippled and diseased animals as offerings to God, animals they wouldn't even want for themselves. And they thought they could get away with it.

These verses sometimes come into my mind when I'm preparing sermons, especially if I've had a very busy week. Then I remind myself that because the King of Kings is with us when we worship, if I were to produce a badly prepared sermon I would be guilty of exactly the same sin as the Israelites. Immediately after Malachi told the people that they were loved he added, *'A son honours his father, and a servant his master. If I am a father, where is the honour due to me? If I am a master, where is the respect due to me?' says the* LORD *Almighty* (1:6).

When the prophet goes on to ask if they would offer damaged sacrifices to the governor, he is saying that they care more about the governor of Persia than they do about God. Why does he say this to them as soon as he assures them they are loved? The answer is that they are loved, but God expects them to honour him as well.

The Israelites had two problems: they didn't feel loved and they didn't honour God. One of the reasons they didn't feel loved was that they were in such a bad state of mind that they couldn't recognise God's love; so far had they backslidden. God would do us no favour not to teach us to love him, and how to love him, just as parents do their children no favour who do not teach respect. We should teach our children the fifth commandment. My father used to quote, *'Honour your father and mother,'* all the time. Some parents are afraid to talk like that. We live in a time when children show very little respect for their parents, and it is partly because their parents have not earned their respect or taught them the need for it.

God, having sent Malachi to say, *'You are loved'*, immediately says, *'If I am a father where is the honour due to me?'* (1:6). Why is this such an important word for today? I believe that when people don't feel loved it is often because they haven't responded to the love of God. Not only that, they have become so self-centred that they cannot even recognise God's love. That was true of the people of Israel. They had become cynical, and cynicism is almost always a sign of backsliding. We need to ask ourselves some serious questions if we become cynical.

Not only had the Israelites become cynical, but they were taking the sacrificial system for granted. Translating that into our present generation we see those who profess faith in Jesus Christ but cannot say for sure that they know they are saved, or why they are saved. On top of that, the priests were bored with their duties. This can happen when church leaders forget why they are there and begin to show no respect for their office or calling. In 450 BC the priests scarcely bothered to maintain the standard of the Mosaic law. God says, *'It is you, O priests, who show contempt for my name'* (1:6). We too are living at a time when church leaders often take the essentials for granted.

Malachi saw other signs of backsliding: tithes weren't being paid, the temple was in disrepair, and people felt there was no profit in serving God. There was intermarriage with pagan Gentiles. Some said that because Jewish women were boring they wanted to divorce them and go outside Israel to find more exotic girls. Jewish women suffered because divorce was widespread.

If God shows that he loves us he wants us to show that we love him, and the Israelites were not doing that. We show that we love the Lord by honouring him. And we honour him by honouring his name. That is why God's charge against the priests is, *'It is you, O priests, who show contempt for my name'* (1:6). God's name is his reputation. A name can also refer to influence. When you fill out a job application, and put somebody's name down who will vouch for you, if that person is respected he will influence your potential employer. A name can refer to authority; some people's names carry authority because of who they are. We honour God by honouring his name. God cares about his name.

Three further points should be taken from these verses. The first is about the location of God's honour, because in verse 6 he asks where the honour is that is due to me ? Where refers to location. So where exactly does God want to be honoured? The answer is that God wants to be honoured wherever we are. He wants to be honoured in our homes. Do we honour God in our homes? He wants to be honoured in our families, in our relationships with our families. Do we do that? He wants to be honoured where we work. When we are on the job, do we honour him? Do we watch the language we use; do we watch our attitude? Remember people are looking at us. If the word were to leak out that you are a Christian, would your colleagues be surprised? Or would they say, 'Well I am not surprised. There is something different about you.'

God wants to be honoured at church. He wants to be honoured through our worship. The thirty minutes or so devoted to worship at the beginning of a service is very important to God, and it should be very important to us too. When we get to heaven I guarantee that we will discover that these thirty minutes are important to God. Sometimes we come to church when everything has gone wrong, somebody has hurt our feelings ten minutes before we walk in the door, or we get bad news, or something just tears us up inside. That is the best time to come to God and say, 'I love you.'

We should also be honouring him by the way we spend our money. How often we wish we could have the money back that we spent on things we'd rather we hadn't bought? Do we honour God by the use of our time? 'Where,' God asks us, 'is the honour due to me?' Where is the honour due when you are on holiday? Do you think God understands you need a break from honouring him? Your Bible doesn't even go with you or, if it does, it just sits there. Where is the honour due to his name when you are alone, when nobody else can see?

Secondly, the leadership and God's honour. There is a saying in the Old Testament 'like priests like people.' Priests were taken from the tribe of Levi. Priests occupied the most prestigious positions in Israel. The tribe of Levi was a class apart. Levites were singularly honoured. Today to be in Christian leadership is the highest privilege in the world, whether deacon, minister, vicar, curate or whatever. In November 1954, I felt for the first time in my life that I was really called to preach. Perhaps I should have known before, but I was waiting for a vision or some audible voice that never came. The real problem was that I was afraid of going into the ministry unless I was called. Charles Spurgeon said, 'If you can do anything else, do it.' James says, *'Not many of you should presume to be teachers, my brothers, because you know that we who teach will be judged more strictly'* (Jas. 3:1). We should ask questions of our church leaders. Does their leadership make you want to draw closer to God? If it doesn't, they have failed you. Is there any part of the Bible they are neglecting? If there is, they have failed you. Does sitting under their ministry cause you to want to honour God? If not, they have failed you.

Thirdly, the law and God's honour. Malachi shows that blemished animals would not be presented to a human governor much less to God. They were giving to God what was of no use to them, in the same way that some people give things to a charity, and get a good feeling from doing it, even though they only give what they don't want themselves. How different it is with God. When he in all his wisdom planned salvation, he planned it perfectly. First, God said, I'll do it myself. Then the second person of the Godhead said, you have prepared for me a body. And God gave Jesus a human body when the Word became flesh. He was without defect, without any spot or blemish. Not only did Jesus come into the world perfect, he also perfectly kept the law. He never sinned in thought, word or deed, never in all of his life. That is why he is fit to be our Saviour.

Having given us his Son, God hates it when people think that they are going to be saved by doing their best or turning over a new leaf, or by being baptised or joining a church. After all that went into the sacrificial system, and the Lamb of God who is the ultimate fulfilment of it, it is an insult to say that anyone can bypass Christ and still go to heaven. The good news is that it doesn't require a perfect faith to be saved, but it does require trust in a perfect Saviour. When you come to the place where you transfer to Christ the trust that you have in your good works, then God says, I'll save you.

4

BEGGING GOD –
WOULD YOU DO IT?

'A son honours his father, and a servant his master. If I am a father, where is the honour due to me? If I am a master, where is the respect due to me?' says the LORD Almighty. 'It is you, O priests, who show contempt for my name. But you ask, "How have we shown contempt for your name?" 'You place defiled food on my altar.' But you ask, "How have we defiled you?" By saying that the LORD's table is contemptible. When you bring blind animals for sacrifice, is that not wrong? When you sacrifice crippled or diseased animals, is that not wrong? Try offering them to your governor! Would he be pleased with you? Would he accept you?' says the LORD Almighty. 'Now implore God to be gracious to us. With such offerings from your hands, will he accept you?' – says the LORD Almighty (Malachi 1:6-9).

When was the last time you begged God for anything? Can you recall a time when you did that? You may say that you have never done anything like that in your life; you may say that the last thing you would ever do is beg God. In fact, you may even say that you would never beg anybody for anything. Or you may assert that God would not expect that of us. Malachi says, *'Now implore God to be gracious to us'* (1:9). The word 'implore' means to plead, to beg, to entreat with earnestness. That is what Malachi counsels Israel to do. There is a touch of irony here. It is very possible that the last thing these people felt like doing was begging to God. The theme of the book of Malachi is, *You are loved*. But they didn't feel loved, in fact they felt let down. They were saying. 'If this is love I can't imagine what it would be like not to be loved, because this doesn't feel like love to me.' They felt that God had let them down. Now to those very people who felt that God had let them down, Malachi says, 'Beg God to be gracious.' I imagine they told him that he must be joking! They may have said, 'Let God beg us; he needs to prove himself. How dare you ask us to beg him.'

Begging is something we do when we are desperate. Only when you have hit the bottom, do you go to a person and ask him to do you a favour. But even that is not begging because you intend to pay him back one day. When you beg, you do so knowing that the other person can give or withhold and there is nothing you can do about it; you have no bargaining power. As long as you have some power you can plea-bargain, 'If you will do this for me I'll do that for you.' But that is not begging; that is making a proposition. When you beg, you are so humble you are actually asking for mercy. Mercy, to be mercy, can be given or withheld and justice be done in either case.

Malachi has told them that they are loved, but he has also told them they aren't showing love for God. In fact, they are dishonouring his name. They are going right against the Levitical law. To offer God sacrifices of crippled or diseased animals was to show contempt for the name of God. Malachi knows that God has been offended and that the only step forward is for these people to go to God on bended knee. That is why he urges them to *'implore God to be gracious'*. Why would he do that? The answer is that they aren't going to feel loved by God until they show love to him. This is a very important point, as the following will explain.

2,000 years ago, God sent the promised Messiah to Israel. But the people missed the promise that belonged to them. Messiah came to them and they didn't even recognise him. Have you ever wondered why? Isaiah, several hundred years in advance of his coming, told Israel exactly what the Messiah would be like. It would seem impossible for them to miss him when he came, especially considering his miracles. How could they miss him when it was so obvious by his works who he was? The answer is that the people of Jesus' day were just like the people Malachi addressed. They felt that God had deserted them, that God didn't love them. And they dishonoured God's name because their state of mind was such they could not recognise the authentic Messiah. Had you asked any Pharisee, chief priest or Sadducee at the time of Jesus, 'Do you think there is any chance that the Messiah could come and you would miss him?' they would have said, 'No, if he comes we'll know him.' But Messiah came and they missed him because they had lost all sense of spiritual discernment.

And there is another reason why Malachi's words are important. Begging God is not only right, it is the only way to approach him. It is the only way anyone is ever converted. You ask for mercy because you know that you don't deserve it. When you ask for mercy you are at the bottom. The words 'God have mercy on me' come from a Greek word that means 'God be propitious'. It is a word that describes the blood sprinkled on the mercy seat that satisfied the justice of God. Whenever you use that word it is like saying, 'God, don't look at me, look at the blood Jesus shed on the cross, and have mercy on me.'

There is a third reason this is important. The people of Israel felt sorry for themselves and they thought that God should come begging to them. The last thing they wanted was for the prophet to tell them they were wrong and that they should be imploring God to be gracious. If you are feeling a little sorry for yourself the only way to come out of it is to go on bended knees and say, 'God, I'm sorry, I'm sorry.'

One last thing needs to be said on this subject. Begging God is what you will do one day. It is only a matter of time. In Jesus' parable of the rich man and Lazarus, when the rich man went to hell he called out, *'Father Abraham, have pity on me and send Lazarus to dip the tip of his finger in water and cool my tongue, because I am in agony in this fire'* (Luke 16:24). Right now there are people begging God just as the rich man did. They were too proud to do it on earth, but they are begging now from hell. If that is where you are at, beg for mercy while there is time.

Malachi knew that his work was not going to be easy because he knew the attitude of the people. I think the most delicate task a pastor has to do is listen to people who believe they are spiritual and who have been maligned and hurt, when in his heart he knows that they are the problem, and that he has to tell them so. Paul says, *'If someone is caught in a sin, you who are spiritual should restore him gently. But watch yourself, or you also may be tempted'* (Gal. 6:1). If you find another person overtaken in a sin, you have to approach him in a very delicate way, remembering that it could happen to you.

Generally speaking, there are two kinds of sins. In the case of overt and obvious sin, the person already knows why you have come to him. You still have to deal with him in a delicate and gentle way, but at least he will admit that there is sin there. The other kind of sin, when the person doesn't think he has done anything wrong, is more difficult. It needs great sensitivity and care. Malachi is facing that most delicate task. The worst kind of backsliders are those who sincerely feel they are in a healthy spiritual state. They don't realise that they have let bitterness creep in. They don't realise they are being judgmental. They just don't see what they are like and what they are doing.

Malachi was addressing people who were guilty of three things. Firstly, the abuse of grace. They were loved by God but they were not honouring his name, that is, they were abusing grace. When God gives you eternal life, he puts you on your honour to show gratitude to him. You abuse his grace when you live in a way that does not bring honour to his name.

Secondly, they were guilty of an absence of gratitude. We get to heaven by asking God to be merciful to us because Jesus died for us on the cross. We honour his name as a way of saying thank you. There are people who think that keeping the Ten Commandments is a precondition of salvation. They are wrong. Striving to obey the Ten Commandments is how we say thank you to God for saving us. God puts us on our honour to live a life that shows we are thankful. Keeping the law of God is like the PS at the end of a letter that says, 'Thank you, thank you.'

Thirdly, the Israelites were guilty of an abundance of greed. They were not content with just what they needed; they wanted more, and jealousy set in.

What was it God wanted of these people? He wanted fellowship with them. He said, 'I love you,' not because he approved, but because he wanted to change them. We will never get anybody to change if we make it a condition of our love. God doesn't do that. He starts off by loving, and his love is the motivation for change.

The most wonderful feeling in the world is knowing that we are loved unconditionally, and that is what God does for us in the gospel. If we had to come up to a set standard in order to be loved, we would never know for sure if we were loved. What Malachi is saying is, 'You do not have to change to be loved, but he loves you so that you will begin to honour his name.' If God loves us, you might ask, why do we have to implore him to be gracious? The answer is that his love for us does not mean that he approves of what we have done. Rather he accepts us in order that we might begin to honour his name. God loves us and wants to delight in us because we return our love to him. It was because Israel was not returning God's love that the prophet told them to go to him on bended knee and beg.

5

Cheap Grace

'Oh, that one of you would shut the temple doors, so that you would not light useless fires on my altar! I am not pleased with you,' says the Lord Almighty, 'and I will accept no offering from your hands. My name will be great among the nations, from the rising to the setting of the sun. In every place incense and pure offerings will be brought to my name, because my name will be great among the nations,' says the Lord Almighty. 'But you profane it by saying of the Lord's table, "It is defiled", and of its food, "It is contemptible." And you say, "What a burden!" and you sniff at it contemptuously,' says the Lord Almighty. 'When you bring injured, crippled or diseased animals and offer them as sacrifices, should I accept them from your hands?' says the Lord. 'Cursed is the cheat who has an acceptable male in his flock and vows to give it, but then sacrifices a blemished animal to the Lord. For I am a great king,' says the Lord Almighty, 'and my name is to be feared among the nations' (Malachi 1:10-14).

God is unhappy with his people and he uses his prophet to tell them so. *'Oh, that one of you would shut the temple doors, so that you would not light useless fires on my altar! I am not pleased with you,' says the Lord Almighty, 'and I will accept no offering from your hands'* (1:10). When we come to church we often just take for granted that God will be there to bless us. But here he says he would prefer no worship than worthless worship. The prophet's message to the people is the same as God's message to us: Get it right or stop it. That is what he is saying to each one of us. Our worship doesn't necessarily please him.

God also has something else to say, and this is so important for us too. ' *"My name will be great among the nations, from the rising to the setting of the sun. In every place incense and pure offerings will be brought to my name, because my name will be great among the nations," says the Lord Almighty'* (1:11).

There were times in the Old Testament era when Israel's relationship was right with God and other nations came to respect him. For example, when Rahab saw the spies coming into Jericho, she said, 'We know about you!' The God of Israel was respected even in Jericho. Nebuchadnezzar respected the God of Israel. Jonah went into Nineveh and the whole nation repented. Cyrus king of Persia set Israel free to go back. But it was very different in Malachi's day. God says, *'You profane it by saying of the Lord's table, "It is defiled", and of its food, "It is contemptible," And you say, "What a burden!" and you sniff at it contemptuously," says the Lord Almighty'* (1:12-13). The people of God are not right with him and the nations outside are not going to have any respect at all.

There is a sense in which as the church goes, so goes the nation. What would happen if people in the world decided to come into the typical church? They would find Christians who don't even speak to each other, people who would turn and walk in another direction if they saw certain others coming. As there are people who need to forgive one another in the church of God, it is no wonder that the world concludes they have no need to fear him. You and I are appalled when our governments pass laws that legalise things that are disgraceful. Should we blame our rulers? We should not. If we were right with God as a church these things would not happen.

The children of Israel had cheapened the grace of God. The sacrificial system was of incalculable value but they had cheapened what was sacred to God. Because they thought they were forgiven, that they didn't have to keep to God's rules, they dishonoured his name. God hates a church that dishonours his name.

This passage also shows how God can love us and be unhappy with us at the same time. Parents know what it is like to love their children and be displeased with them at the same time. And God's children are no different from ours. There are many backsliders, people who have been converted but who have slipped, who do things they would once never have dreamt of doing. They play fast and loose with the things of the world; their glow has gone and their love for Christ has waned. They are loved but God is unhappy. God wants to be honoured in the church in order that the world might see and honour him, but the church keeps it from happening. Cheap grace neither honours God nor does the people any good.

When the time came for God to offer the perfect sacrifice to which all of the Old Testament sacrifices pointed, he sent his best; he sent his Son, the Lamb without spot or blemish. And God wants our best in return. *'Therefore, I urge you, brothers, in view of God's mercy, to offer your bodies as living sacrifices, holy and pleasing to God – this is your spiritual act of worship'* (Rom. 12:1). That means we have to give some things up, to sacrifice things for his honour and glory. That's not fun, and it may not be easy, but we do it. Why? When we consider what God has done for us, it is a small thing. We don't do it in order to be saved; we don't do it in order to buy our way to heaven. We do it in order to say, 'Thank you, thank you for saving me.'

Grace is undeserved favour from God. It is seen when God just decides to bless you, giving you what you don't deserve. You deserve him to throw the book at you, but instead he says, 'I am going to bless you.' But what is cheap grace? Cheap grace is presuming to have his love without any regard for God himself. Cheap grace is having a relationship with God that costs nothing. The Israelites cheapened grace by giving him sacrifices that cost them nothing. Genuine faith is when you recognize that God has offered the perfect sacrifice and you begin to feel convicted, you are so sorry that you beg God to wash your sins away by his blood.

Three things remain to be said on this subject. The first is what I like to call the irony of grace. Irony is like a paradox, contradictory but true. The irony of grace is this: grace is not cheap, it is free. *'It is by grace you have been saved, through faith - and this not from yourselves, it is the gift of God – not by works, so that no-one can boast'* (Eph. 2:8-9). Yet the other irony is that it is not cheap, it costs you everything. Isaac Watt's hymn says, 'Love so amazing, so divine, demands my soul, my life, my all.' The irony is that the entrance is by free faith alone, but for the annual fee God wants all of you. He says, Now I have freely saved you, here is what I want of you.

Secondly, the intent of grace, or its purpose. Why is Malachi talking like this to the people? God wanted to show love for the people even though they didn't deserve it, and he wants to do the same today. He has enough on any one of us to bury us, yet he is saying, Grace, grace, but not cheap grace. The intent of grace is not only to show love when we don't deserve it, but to produce changed lives, hearts full of gratitude, believers bringing honour to God in order that the world out there will respect him. It was said of Mary, Queen of Scots that she feared the prayers of John Knox more than an army of 10,000 men.

Thirdly, the initiation of grace which is proof that God is at work. What separates true and false religion? By false I mean natural religion, and all other religions too. What separates the Christian faith from every other religion on earth, whether Jehovah's Witnesses' beliefs or Mormonism or Islam or Buddhism or New Age thinking? What separates them is the author of the process of belief. Only God initiates true faith. In other words, we cannot make faith happen, only God can. This was the bottom line, this was why God was angry. After all he had done for them, how dare they do what they were doing! *'Cursed is the cheat who has an acceptable male in his flock and vows to give it, but then sacrifices a blemished animal to the Lord'* (1:14).

This describes someone who in a moment of panic says, 'Lord, if you will get me through this I'll give you the best animal I've got.' Then the crisis subsides, and he thinks. 'It was a bit hasty to promise to give that to the Lord,' and goes and finds an injured one. Maybe you have made a promise to God in circumstances like that then, when the trouble passed, you decided that it would have passed anyway. That makes God angry.

God knew from the foundation of the world that he would send his Son, the Lamb of God without spot or blemish. Until the time came for Jesus to be born, God insisted that every sacrifice should be without defect because it pointed to his Son. And here they come offering diseased animals! God says, No you don't! The good news is that even though they cheapened grace God sent his Son, the perfect sacrifice, for our salvation. Saving grace is not cheap, it is free; it is free to those who are bought by the blood of the Lamb.

6

TAKING GOD FOR GRANTED

'Oh, that one of you would shut the temple doors, so that you would not light useless fires on my altar! I am not pleased with you,' says the LORD Almighty, 'and I will accept no offering from your hands. My name will be great among the nations, from the rising to the setting of the sun. In every place incense and pure offerings will be brought to my name, because my name will be great among the nations,' says the LORD Almighty. 'But you profane it by saying of the Lord's table, "It is defiled", and of its food, "It is contemptible." And you say, "What a burden!" and you sniff at it contemptuously,' says the LORD Almighty. 'When you bring injured, crippled or diseased animals and offer them as sacrifices, should I accept them from your hands?' says the LORD. 'Cursed is the cheat who has an acceptable male in his flock and vows to give it, but then sacrifices a blemished animal to the Lord. For I am a great king,' says the LORD Almighty, 'and my name is to be feared among the nations' (Malachi 1:10-14).

The expression 'to take for granted' means to assume something is true or sure to happen. Or it means to be so sure of having something that we no longer appreciate it. That is what this passage is about. The words are addressed to the priesthood, that is the equivalent in the Old Testament of what we might call the paid clergy. It is the highest honour in the world to be called to preach. But this section of Malachi is addressed to those who were called to preach by virtue of their birth. They didn't respond to a call to preach as we do today; they were in the full-time ministry simply because they were born into the tribe of Levi.

The thing that particularly grips me about this passage is that God notices. These professional clergymen had actually given God animals they couldn't use themselves. They thought that God wouldn't notice and didn't care. But he did notice. He sees everything we do. Jesus said, *'There is nothing concealed that will not be disclosed, or hidden that will not be made known. What you have said in the dark will be said in the daylight, and what you have whispered in the ear in the inner rooms will be proclaimed from the housetops'* (Luke 12:2-3). If we really believed that, we would watch every word we say. Elsewhere Jesus said, *'I tell you that men will have to give account on the day of judgment for every careless word they have spoken'* (Matt. 12:36). That verse makes me want to live my life again. God notices everything we do and these verses make that quite clear.

This word is not just for preachers; it is for every believer, because every believer is part of the body of Christ. For some reason we seem to think that God will make allowances for us, that he knows our situations and will understand our failures. But here we learn that God not only noticed what was happening, but he was angry about it. He didn't let the priests get away with what they were doing, and he won't let us away with taking him for granted either.

Four points need to be made. Firstly, an ungrateful ministry. These men were in a position of privilege. They were Jews. The Jew is given a head start. He is acquainted with things that the world generally doesn't know about. But the highest privilege was not only to be born a Jew, but to be born into the tribe of Levi. That was the equivalent of being born into a Christian home.

My background was very strict. I wasn't allowed to go to the cinema or do certain other things, and I had to go to church every time the door was opened. I grew up wondering why I had to do all these things when my friend across the street did not. Now I thank God that I was born into a Christian home and called into the ministry, even though from those who have been given much, much will be demanded. But many who have been entrusted with great blessings are like those in the priesthood who became bored with church, bored with the service of the Lord. They took it for granted, and their ingratitude in taking God for granted was a great sin.

How do we know God was upset with them for taking him for granted? He felt so strongly about it that he said he would prefer they stopped worshipping at all. *'Oh, that one of you would shut the temple doors, so that you would not light useless fires upon my altar!'* (1:10). He would prefer that the doors of the church were closed than for this mockery to continue. I am sure that the same is true of those in the clergy today, whatever denomination, whatever training, whatever education, whatever level of intelligence, who are not preaching God's word. He would rather they stopped preaching than preach no gospel. Anyone who doesn't preach the gospel should resign his charge and get a job working in a supermarket rather than profane God's word by denying it. God says, *'Oh, that one of you would shut the doors, so that you would not light useless fires on **my** altar!* (1:10). That is the key: it is *God's* altar, his service, *his* work, *his* worship and they are looking at it as *theirs.*

In addition to all these things the priests in Malachi's day had forgotten the magnitude of God's glory. God tells them, *'My name will be great among the nations'* (1:11). God wanted Israel to be so focused on him that through his people's worship the whole world would fear the Lord. He wants his name to be great in the world today. What are we doing to contribute to that? These people thought only of themselves; they thought they were God's only interest. The truth is that God has determined that one day, *'Every knee should bow, in heaven and on earth and under the earth, and every tongue confess that Jesus Christ is Lord, to the glory of God the Father'* (Phil. 2:10-11).

If you are engaged in ministry, whether you are a deacon or involved in children's work, doing the flowers or sweeping the floors, helping with the food or taking someone to church, and you are saying, 'What a burden,' and you are bored with it, don't you realise what a privilege God has given to you to do anything in his name?

The second thing is unconscious motivation. What was the people's unconscious motivation? It was self-righteousness. They actually felt that they were doing God a favour! If you think you are doing God a favour because you go to church, God would rather you stayed at home! If you think you are doing God a favour by putting money in the collection or giving to charity, God would rather you kept it for yourself. God doesn't want or need our favours. They make him angry.

You will never be a Christian until you come to the place where you recognise that, far from being able to do anything for God, you don't deserve the least of his grace. As long as you feel you deserve better from God than he has given you, you are not saved. The people who are saved are those who realise they were lost and on their road to hell when God stopped them in their tracks and showed them that Jesus died for them. When the Holy Spirit showed them their sin, the last thought in their minds was that they could do God a favour!

The third thing about this passage is unthinkable murmurings. The Israelites did not only have ungodly thoughts, but they verbalised their feelings. They were saying that the Lord's table was contemptible. What a contrast in chapter three. *'Those who feared the LORD talked with each other, and the LORD listened and heard'* (3:16).

One last point is their ultimate miscalculation. They thought they would get away with it. These people really believed that their thoughts and their words weren't being heard, and that God wouldn't notice their substandard sacrifices. Wrong! God heard and saw it all; he stepped in and he was angry. How dare they dishonour God's name! How dare they take him for granted! And what a warning to us.

7

WHEN THE CHURCH DOES
MORE HARM THAN GOOD

'And now this admonition is for you, O priests. If you do not listen, and if you do not set you heart to honour my name,' says the LORD Almighty, 'I will send a curse upon you, and I will curse your blessings. Yes, I have already cursed them, because you have not set your heart to honour me. Because of you I will rebuke your descendants, I will spread on your face the offal from your festival sacrifices, and you will be carried off with it. And you will know that I have sent you this admonition so that my covenant with Levi may continue,' says the LORD Almighty. 'My covenant was with him, a covenant of life and peace, and I gave them to him; this called for reverence and he revered me and stood in awe of my name. True instruction was in his mouth and nothing false was found on his lips. He walked with me in peace and uprightness, and turned many from sin. For the lips of a priest ought to preserve knowledge, and from his mouth men should seek instruction – because he is the messenger of the LORD Almighty. But you have turned from the way and by your teaching have caused many to stumble; you have violated the covenant with Levi,' says the LORD Almighty. 'So I have caused you to be despised and humiliated before all the people, because you have not followed my ways but have shown partiality in matters of the law' (2:1-9).

Jonathan Edwards is regarded as America's greatest theologian, and he was without doubt the leading figure in the Great Awakening from 1725 to 1750. At the height of the Great Awakening in 1741, Edwards preached a sermon that, when it went to press, was given the title, 'Sinners in the Hands of an Angry God'. There was so much of the Spirit's power present when that sermon was preached that hundreds of people literally clung to tree trunks outside the church and held on to church pews inside to keep themselves from falling into hell. So great was the power of God. The words on Jonathan Edward's tomb are, *'The law of truth was in his mouth, and iniquity was not found on his lips. He walked with me in peace and equity and did turn many away from iniquity'* (2:6 AV). Nothing greater could be said about anyone.

This verse refers to the time when Aaron allowed the people to make, out of gold, a calf that they then bowed down and worshipped. *'Moses saw that the people were running wild and that Aaron had let them get out of control and so become a laughing-stock to their enemies. So he stood at the entrance to the camp and said, "Whoever is for the Lord, come to me." And all the Levites rallied to him'* (EX. 32:25-26). I think it was as a result of that incident that God made the tribe of Levi the most prestigious in ancient Israel. Levites were given the privilege of handling the worship and maintaining the sacrificial system. That is why Malachi could say of them, *'The lips of the priest ought to preserve knowledge, and from his mouth men should seek instruction – because he is the messenger of the LORD Almighty'* (2:7). That should describe any minister of the gospel and any church leader.

Sadly these words did not describe the priesthood in Malachi's day and God was so upset. I have had times in my life when God made it clear he was upset with me. That's an awful feeling, but nothing in comparison with what it would be like to stand before God on the day when I am required to give an account of my life. In this passage God was upset with the leadership in Israel. What does that have to do with us? It shows us the responsibility of leadership, and what happens when that leadership is irresponsible. Winston Churchill said that the price of greatness is responsibility. And as the leadership, so goes the church; as the church, so goes the nation. Jesus said, *'You are the salt of the earth. But if the salt loses its saltiness, how can it be made salty again? It is no longer good for anything, except to be thrown out and trampled by men'* (Matt. 5:13). That was exactly the problem Malachi addressed.

The people of Israel were suffering and oppressed, and the reason for that was their leadership. This partly explains why the church today is in a mess. Four to five per cent of people attend church in the UK and that includes Protestant and Roman Catholic, even Mormons and Jehovah's Witnesses. If you were to ask how many of those are Bible-believing Christians, the percentage would be even lower. We are living in a time when there is a form of godliness but a denial of power, when church leaders applaud what was once shamed, whether it be adultery, homosexual practice, lying or stealing. The most elementary kinds of righteousness are now repudiated by those in leadership. Respect for the church in general, and the clergy in particular, is at an all-time low.

We had a rude awakening when we first went to England. Although I had been told it wasn't quite like America as far as there being no Bible Belt was concerned, I wasn't prepared for the vast difference. I could just sense the godless atmosphere. Our daughter was asked by her friend's mother what her father did. She told her I was a minister. The woman said, 'You mean a minister of a church? How long has he done that?' When my daughter explained I'd only ever been a minister, the woman replied, 'You mean he has never had a proper job!' What a way to look at the clergy.

I saw a poll some years ago that showed the respect people had for different professions. Taxi drivers had a higher standing than clergymen. Time was when it was the minister of the gospel who was held in esteem. That was because *'true instruction was in their mouths, nothing false was found on their lips, and they walked with God in peace'* (2:6). A hundred years has brought us from that to where we are today. We've gone a long way from the Jonathan Edwards and John Wesleys of this world. Wesley got up at four o'clock every morning and prayed for two hours before beginning the day. A recent UK poll of all church leaders showed that they spent an average of four minutes a day in quiet time! John Wesley spent two hours a day, Martin Luther spent two hours a day. Jonathan Edwards was a man who was on his knees constantly - and we wonder why the church is powerless!

What has this got to do with us? It shows what we have a right to expect when we embrace the God of the Bible. We should expect from the church the leadership that God intended. We have a right to the kind of spiritual leadership Malachi envisages here. But there is a second reason this word applies to you who sit in the pew, and that is that you are guilty if you tolerate anything else. If you go along with a Bible-denying ministry, you are also guilty. Some say, 'Well my pastor may not preach the Bible but he is a very nice person.' That may well be, but God will judge you if that's the situation you are in and you don't do something about it.

When does a church do more harm than good? Firstly, when its leadership doesn't listen to the Lord. *'"This admonition is for you, O priests. If you do not listen, and if you do not set your hearts to honour my name," says the LORD Almighty, "I will send a curse upon you, and I will curse your blessings"'* (2:1). That is an awful thing, when the vicar or the priest or the pastor stands up at the end of the service and says, 'The grace of our Lord Jesus Christ, the love of God and the blessing of the Holy Spirit be with you,' and God turns the blessing into a curse. Because the people Malachi addressed were under a curse it was no wonder they didn't feel loved. Everything was going wrong and the prophet admonished the priests. Then came a word to all the rest, telling them that because they were also responsible before God they could not pass the buck. Remember, in the

New Testament there is no distinction between priesthood and laity, we are all part of the priesthood of all believers.

Secondly, a church does more harm than good when its leaders do not turn people from evil to good. Any teaching that does not promote godly living is false. The proof that preaching is sound is that people have an aspiration for the honour and glory of God. No wonder God said he wished somebody would close the doors!

Thirdly, a church does more harm than good when its leadership does not preserve teaching. This comes as a surprise to a lot of people. What do you suppose was the chief function of the ancient priests? You may have thought it was offering the sacrifices. Wrong. *'The lips of the priest ought to preserve knowledge'* (2:7). Why go to church? We go to be taught, to get instruction. That is why we had the School of Theology on Fridays in Westminster Chapel. We tried to make it simple so that people could know what they were to believe.

Fourthly, the church does more harm than good when people will not seek instruction. *'From his mouth men should seek instruction'* (2:7). We should want instruction; we should desire to know God's Word. And where there are those who call themselves the people of God, but who are not seeking instruction, it is no wonder the church does more harm than good. *'I have caused you to be despised and humiliated before the people'* (2:9). Oxford University was founded on the motto 'The Lord is my Life' because it was God-centred. In those days the study of theology was its great aim, now it is the study of science. God says though Malachi, *'I will spread on your faces the offal from your festival sacrifices'* (2:3). That means taking the intestines from the animal offerings and rubbing them on the faces of the priests.

The objective of the priesthood is twofold: to set an example and to teach. God says that those who represent him have to practise what they preach. He goes on, *"'You will know that I*

have sent you this admonition so that my covenant with Levi
may continue," says the LORD Almighty' (2:4). God, in his
overruling providence, was going to do away with that generation
of priests and start all over again because he had made a covenant
with Levi that would be fulfilled when Jesus died on the cross.

The people were given an opportunity to turn from sin. 'He
walked with me in peace and uprightness, and turned many from
sin' (2:6). Turning from doing things that dishonour God is not
what saves us, but it does show that something has happened.
When we invite Jesus Christ to come into our hearts, he gives
us a new appetite, a new affection. We should walk in the light
and lighten up the darkness around us.

8

Should a Christian Marry a Non-Christian?

Have we not all one Father? Did not one God create us? Why do we profane the covenant of our fathers by breaking faith with one another? Judah has broken faith. A detestable thing has been committed in Israel and in Jerusalem: Judah has desecrated the sanctuary the Lord loves, by marrying the daughter of a foreign god. As for the man who does this, whoever he may be, may the Lord cut him off from the tents of Jacob – even though he brings offerings to the Lord Almighty' (Malachi 2:10-12).

In ancient Israel there were laws as well as traditions against marrying foreign women. The first indication of this was Abraham's instruction to his servant, *'I want you to swear by the Lord, the God of heaven and the God of earth, that you will not get a wife for my son from the daughters of the Canaanites, among whom I am living, but will go to my country and my own relatives and get a wife for my son Isaac'* (Gen. 24:3). God says, *'Be careful not to make a treaty with those who live in the land … and when you choose some of their daughters as wives for your sons and those daughters prostitute themselves to their gods, they will lead your sons to do the same'* (Gen. 34:15-16). *'Do not intermarry with them. Do not give your daughters to their sons or take their daughters for your sons, for they will turn your sons way from following me to serve other gods, and the Lord's anger will burn against you and will quickly destroy you'* (Deut. 7:3-4).

In the sight of God, when a man has intercourse with a woman they are then one flesh. More than the sexual urge is involved; it is something spiritual, it is an act of commitment. At the time of Nehemiah, when the men of Israel began marrying foreign women and having children by them, the prophet recognised how angry God was. The exile into Babylon had resulted from Israel's falling away, and partly for this very reason. Then, when the people were restored to their own land, they began doing exactly the same thing again! There was only one thing to do, and I have to admit that every year when I come to that passage in my Bible reading plan my heart goes out to the people even though it happened hundreds of years ago, they had to return their wives and children back to where they came from. It was a heartbreaking thing to do, but it was the only way to restore God's honour in the nation. Because it was unthinkable to Malachi that the whole nation would be put at risk yet again for the same sin, he used the strongest words.

Why is this passage important today? Firstly, it shows that God has strong feelings about who believers should marry. I am so grateful that I had a father who prayed from my earliest days that I would not fall in love with a non-Christian girl. It was a shrewd prayer, because Dad knew that it was too late to try to reason once a man and woman are in love. Marriage is God's idea. *'For this reason a man will leave his father and mother and be united to his wife, and they will become one flesh'* (Gen. 2:24), but it is a gift that comes with the Maker's rules. Sexual intercourse makes a man and woman one flesh.

There is a second reason this is an important word. In order to live happily together a married couple must have a common understanding in matters of faith. You need to find theological and spiritual fellowship. What you believe about the Bible and the things of God needs to be worked out before you fall deeply in love because otherwise it will be swept under the carpet. Don't say that you'll sort out 'all these little things' after you are married, because it almost never happens like that.

This is important, thirdly, because experience has shown overwhelmingly that the Bible is right. The person with a non-biblical religion almost invariably drags the other down. You say, 'I will convert him/her.' Wrong! It just doesn't happen that way. I knew of a young Christian lady who, while backslidden, married a Moslem. When she wanted to come back to the Lord, her husband would not let her. In fact, she had to tiptoe out of their home to come to speak to me. That's how free she was.

Remember Solomon. He *'loved many foreign women ... from nations about which the LORD had told the Israelites, "You must not intermarry with them, because they will surely turn your hearts after their gods." ... As Solomon grew old, his wives turned his heart after other gods, and his heart was not fully devoted to the LORD his God'* (I Kings 11:1-2,4). God didn't even bend the rules for Solomon, David's son. *'The LORD became angry with Solomon because his heart had turned away from the LORD, the God of Israel, who had appeared to him twice. Although he had forbidden Solomon to follow other gods, Solomon did not keep the LORD's command. So the LORD said to Solomon, "Since this is your attitude and you have not kept my covenant and my decrees, which I commanded you, I will most certainly tear the kingdom away from you and give it to one of your subordinates'* (I Kings 11:9-10).

If our sexual drive is not kept under control all kinds of regrettable things will happen. God made us sexual beings. Sex is a physical need as well as a psychological one. Dr Clyde Narramore, Christian psychologist, says that sex was not born in Hollywood but at the throne of grace. It was God's idea. Martin Luther said that God uses sex to drive a man to marriage, ambition to drive a man to service, and fear to drive a man to faith. Billy Graham told a friend of mine, 'It seems that the devil gets seventy-five percent of God's best through sexual temptation.' The sad history of Solomon should be a warning to us.

Three final points. Firstly, God's people are part of a spiritual family. Notice how Malachi puts it, *'Have we not all one Father?'* (2:10). Some think the word Father should have a small 'f', that it is referring to Abraham; Isaiah 51:2 refers to Abraham as their father. Others think it could refer to Jacob from whom all the twelve tribes descended. But it probably means God the Father because it goes on, *'Did not one God create us?'* (2:10). Whichever interpretation we use we are a family under God, a spiritual family. Although family ties are strong, there are many, many Christians who would testify that their real friends are those in their spiritual family. Only a very foolish Christian will not make God's friends his friends. To make best friends with the world is to court disaster.

Secondly, sin in the family. Why was marrying a foreign woman called a detestable thing? It wasn't because of racial prejudice; there is no racial prejudice in God. Not was it because of colour; God made all colours of skin. It was for theological and spiritual reasons. Because Judah was the chosen tribe through which Messiah would come, tribal purity, maintained only by Jewish men marrying Jewish women, was very important. God was then, and is now, concerned about the honour and glory of his name. What was the motivation for marrying outside of the Jewish 'family'? Surprise, surprise, it was sex.

When someone asked Julian Huxley, the evolutionist, why he thought that evolution caught on so quickly, he replied, 'We all jumped at Darwin's, *The Origin of Species,* because the idea of God interfered with our sexual way of life.' People will tell you that they believe in evolution because they are governed by science. That's nonsense. They are governed by their libido. They know that the God of the Bible wants sexual purity, and if it can be proved somehow that evolution is true they are free to live as they choose. No wonder they want it to be true!

Louise and I were invited to the Soviet Union before the collapse of Communism. On a tour through the Hermitage in what was then called Leningrad, I began to talk to the lady who gave us lectures on Rembrandt. When we saw his painting of Moses I asked her what she knew about Moses. It wasn't a lot. She had heard of him but didn't know much about him. After the tour was over, I began to present the gospel to her. I thought, this is marvellous, she is listening to me, as her eyes filled with tears. I was so excited. When we reached the point where I asked her if she would like to receive God's free gift of salvation, her answer was, 'No, because I don't want to give up my boyfriend.' I hadn't said a word about that but the Holy Spirit had. God won't bend the rules, and they are all for our good. But those who put God first will not be sorry.

The last point is that there comes a time when a church has to put a person out of membership. This happened in Corinth when a man who was obviously converted was having a sexual relationship with his stepmother. Excommunication is the last resort, but it sometimes has to be done to maintain the purity of the body of Christ. That person was truly saved but was in a backslidden state. He was eventually restored. God is married to the backslider, but a backslider is of little or no use when he is in that condition. God calls for repentance.

Some final points. One, don't marry a non-Christian. God's word says, *'Do not be yoked together with unbelievers. For what do righteousness and wickedness have in common? Or what fellowship can light have with darkness? What harmony is there between Christ and Belial? What does a believer have in common with an unbeliever? What agreement is there between the temple of God and idols? For we are the temple of the living God. As God has said, "I will live with them and walk among them, and I will be their God, and they will be my people." "Therefore come out from them and be separate," says the Lord. "Touch no unclean thing, and I will receive you. I will be a Father to you and you will be my sons and daughters," says the Lord Almighty'* (2 Cor. 6:14-18).

Two, Don't even date a non-Christian, pray for his/her conversion first or look elsewhere. If you say, 'Well she is not saved but I believe I can lead her to the Lord,' I admit that has happened, and I thank God for when it has. But for every case that it has happened you can find ten horror stories where it has not.

Three, wait on God's choice for you. If it is God's will for you to be married then he has your young woman or man somewhere, and she or he is worth waiting for. What God wants for you is what is best for you.

Four, put Jesus first in your life. Whatever has happened in the past, put him first in the present and the future. That's the obedience he wants from us.

9

When Tears Don't Help

Another thing you do: You flood the LORD's altar with tears. You weep and wail because he no longer pays attention to your offerings or accepts them with pleasure from your hands. You ask, 'Why?' It is because the LORD is acting as the witness between you and the wife of your youth, because you have broken faith with her, though she is your partner, the wife of your marriage covenant' (Malachi 2:13-14).

It is very interesting that we don't often get a quick answer to our Whys. It is possible that we will eventually see at least part of the reason for some of our sufferings, but I have lived long enough to know that although I don't know the reasons for what happens to me, what Paul said in Romans 8:28 is true. *'In all things God works for the good of those who love him, who have been called according to his purpose.'* That is probably the most encouraging verse in the Bible.

Although we can see times when God permitted suffering and we were all the better for it, the bigger question of why he permits evil or suffering in the world at all will not be answered in this life. It will be answered by God himself when, at the final judgment, he clears his name and all see the truth. I believe he will then do it simply, with just one stroke, so that our immediate reaction will be, 'Why didn't I think of that?' One reason he doesn't give the answer to the problem of evil and suffering is in order that we might have faith. God wants us to believe, and belief means not having the evidence but believing anyway.

While we don't have the answer to these great questions, Malachi was able to give an immediate answer to the questions the children of Israel were asking. *'You weep and wail because God no longer pays attention to your offerings or accepts them with pleasure from your hands. You ask, "Why?"'* (2:13-14). Malachi answers immediately, *'It is because the LORD is acting as the witness between you and the wife of your youth'* (2:14). Have you been nice to the wife of your youth? You may say, 'You don't know what she is like. You don't know what I have lived with.' God witnesses; he knows. Has your husband not been very good to you and are you hurting deep inside? God knows.

These people brought goats, lambs and bulls, shedding their blood in order that God would look on their sacrifice, pass over their sin and give them prosperity. But when he didn't accept their offerings and bless them, they flooded the Lord's altar with tears, and all because they had broken faith with the wives of their youth. They were adding sin to sin. First, they married foreign wives. Then they divorced their wives in order to marry other women! And when God didn't prosper them they wept crocodile tears. When a crocodile is getting ready to strike its prey, excitement makes its tears flow. There is no sorrow involved at all, just excitement.

Why were they weeping at the altar? Was there a reason that they didn't just weep at home but went instead to the altar to weep? I think they did it because it was well known in Israel that tears got God's attention. The first time we have the word 'tears' in the Old Testament is when Isaiah the prophet came to King Hezekiah after the king had been told he was going to die. God's message through Isaiah was, *'I have heard your prayer and seen your tears; I will heal you'* (2 Kings 20:5). There is what some Bible scholars call the law of first mention, where the first use of a word in Scripture determines its meaning throughout. The first time tears are mentioned they got God's attention. Tears worked. Women know that tears often work with their husbands. I can endure almost anything, but if my wife cries it drives me crazy and I immediately want to know what it is she wants. The Israelites didn't shed their tears at home, they went public and stood around the altar where they thought God would see them most clearly.

David said, *'Those who sow in tears will reap with songs of joy. He who goes out weeping, carrying seed to sow, will return with songs of joy, carrying sheaves with him'* (Ps. 126:5-6). Tears worked there too, and the Israelites knew it. It was as though God saw the people weeping and decided he had to do something. When Jesus was in Nain, he saw a widow woman about to bury her only son. Jesus, who just couldn't take it when he saw her weeping as she followed the coffin, raised the boy from the dead. Tears move the heart of God. However, this time it wasn't working and the men of Israel couldn't understand why. Malachi explained to them that it was because they had broken faith with the wives of their youth.

As far as they were concerned two things were not working, their tears and their daily sacrifices. What were the daily sacrifices? In the Old Testament you had animal sacrifices that anticipated a day when they would be fulfilled in Jesus Christ who was the sacrificial Lamb of God. When Jesus died on the cross, he shed his blood that we might be saved and go to heaven when we die. His was a once-for-all atonement. That is the first way in which we are to understand the shedding of blood. It refers to being saved. One of my favourite hymns says, 'I need no other argument; I need no other plea. It is enough that Jesus died, and that he died for me.' The Old Testament Day of Atonement prefigured what Jesus would do on the cross.

But there is a second way to understand the shedding of blood, and that is related to continued fellowship with God. Not only would Israel be saved but she would also enjoy fellowship with God. Here Malachi is not talking about the sacrifices that refer to their being saved, but to those relating to continued fellowship with God. *'If we walk in the light, as he is in the light, we have fellowship with one another, and the blood of Jesus, his Son, purifies us from every sin'* (1 John 1:7). If you have ever put your trust in the blood of Jesus you are eternally saved. Once saved, always saved.

I've had people come into the vestry doubting their salvation. I may not know if they are saved, but I do know that those who transfer their trust from good works and put that trust in the blood of Jesus are eternally saved. But it is possible to be saved and not have fellowship with the Lord. When John says that the blood of Jesus purifies us from all sin, he bases it on the condition that we walk in the light. Salvation is forever but fellowship with God is conditional. That's what the Israelites didn't grasp. They were not enjoying fellowship with God, who was, in fact, hiding his face from them. They were not enjoying any kind of prosperity; everything was going wrong. So they thought they would get God's attention by going to the altar and shedding a lot of tears, weeping and wailing.

What does this have to say to us? Firstly, sin and fellowship with God don't mix. Secondly, it is important as it may suggest the reason your prayers don't seem to be being answered although God can overrule and take the most unworthy person and just bless him. We are not talking about being perfect; perfection is not expected. We are talking about living in deliberate sin, refusing to walk in the light. You cannot have it both ways, you cannot have the blood cleansing you then deliberately choose not to walk in the light.

In 1982, God showed me I had to start the Pilot Light Ministry and I had to be one of those taking part in that outreach work. It would have been one thing for me to tell others that I wanted them to go out on the streets, but quite another accepting that God wanted that done and he wanted me to head it. Had I not done that, I have no doubt I would not have stayed the minister of London's Westminster Chapel for more than six months. God would have removed me one way or another. I had to do it. I had to walk in the light God had given me.

Thirdly, weeping is of no value if you continue in disobedience. You may cry, you may wail, you may even be beside yourself with hopelessness and despair, but it is all of no value if you continue in disobedience.

Fourthly, weeping while walking in obedience, combined with the blood being applied, gets God's attention. If you are weeping as you walk in the light, and the bent of your life is to please him - even though you are not perfect - those are the tears that move the heart of God. Tears are no substitute for obedience. In and of themselves they are not a sign of piety. There have been times in the history of the church when people thought they could be saved by the shedding of their tears.

But tears will make no difference at all if they are shed too late. That is an awful truth. *'If you had responded to my rebuke, I would have poured out my heart to you and made my thoughts known to you. But since you rejected me when I called and no-one gave heed when I stretched out my hand, since you ignored all my advice and would not accept my rebuke, I in turn will laugh at your disaster; I will mock when calamity overtakes you – when calamity overtakes you like a storm, when disaster sweeps over you like a whirlwind, when distress and troubles overwhelm you. Then they will call to me but I will not answer; they will look for me but will not find me'* (Pro. 1:23-28). As you read this there is weeping and wailing and gnashing of teeth going on in hell, but those who weep there are shedding their tears too late.

10

WHEN GOD
ROLLS UP HIS SLEEVES

*Another thing you do: You flood the LORD's altar with tears. You weep
and wail because he no longer pays attention to your offerings or
accepts them with pleasure from your hands. You ask, 'Why?' It is
because the LORD is acting as the witness between you and the wife of
your youth, because you have broken faith with her, though she is
your partner, the wife of your marriage covenant. Has not the LORD
made them one? In flesh and spirit they are his. And why one? Because
he was seeking godly offspring. So guard yourself in your spirit, and
do not break faith with the wife of your youth. 'I hate divorce,' says
the LORD God of Israel, 'and I hate a man's covering himself with
violence as with his garment,' says the LORD Almighty' (Malachi 2:13-16).*

A further reason that God pays no attention to your tears
and sacrifices, Malachi tells the Israelites, is that he is *'acting
as the witness between you and the wife of your youth because
you have broken faith with her.'* How would you feel if God were
not answering your prayers, though you cried out again and
again in tears. You might say, 'Surely God is listening. Surely he
knows what I am feeling and he will be touched. Surely he will
step in.'

But although you are doing all of these things, instead of
God answering your prayer things seem to be getting even worse.
And then you are told God is at work after all, but not in the way
you wanted him to be, that instead of vindicating you he is
vindicating somebody else. How would that make you feel? That

is exactly what was happening here, said Malachi. *'You flood the LORD's altar with tears. You weep and wail because he no longer pays attention to your offerings or accepts them with pleasure from your hands. You ask, "Why?"* (2:13-14). I can tell you, says Malachi, it is because the Lord is at work. And he is making sure you understand that he has decided to answer prayer, other people's prayers, people who are praying because you have hurt them. While they are praying out of the hurts you caused them, you are demanding to know why God isn't answering you. But the Lord says that there are others praying who hurt far more deeply than you do, more than you can possibly know.

While the men of Israel's prayers were not being answered, God was listening to their wives, women who had been divorced by husbands who then went outside of Israel to find more exotic young women. These poor women were crying out to God. 'Why have you let this happen to me?' Their husbands wouldn't have believed you if you had told them they were doing wrong because they thought they had biblical support for what they did. If you questioned them, they would misquote from the book of Deuteronomy, and tell you that if a man finds his wife displeasing he can write her a certificate of divorce and send her from his house.

Readers of this book have probably not done what these men did, but perhaps you have hurt your wife deeply by things you have done and said and you still expect God to hear and answer you, while behind the scenes your wife is praying even harder than you are. She too is weeping, and it may be that God is listening to her rather than you. If that is what is happening, God has decided to roll up his sleeves and come to the rescue of someone who has been hurt, oppressed and let down. And that theme runs right through the Bible. God is for the underdog. God is for the person who has been hurt, abused, walked over, stepped on. He is for the man or woman who silently cries out, 'Lord are you there?' And that is what was going on in ancient Israel.

All of us have a story to tell. We have all been hurt, mistreated and misunderstood. Many times the one who hurt you was a Christian, perhaps your own husband or wife. Perhaps what you want most in the world is to be vindicated. When you have been accused of something, and you know you are not guilty, you want people to see you are not guilty. You want to be vindicated, to have your name cleared. Instead of focusing upon your hurt and how you want to be vindicated, I want you to ask whether you have hurt somebody else. How many of you are willing to admit that you have hurt another person who may be saying to the Lord, 'How long, how long, how long?' and have you in mind. And if you knew what they were praying you might even deny having hurt them at all.

Let me put it another way; most people I have had to forgive do not believe that they have done anything that deserves my forgiveness. The worst thing I could do would be to go to this person or that and say, 'I forgive you for what you've done,' because they wouldn't know what I was talking about. What do you do in a case like that? You have to forgive them in your heart, you have to refuse to be bitter, then release them and ask God to bless them. The point I'm making is that when I realise that the people I have had to forgive don't think they've done anything wrong, it stands to reason that I have hurt others without knowing it. In some cases, when I am shown how I have hurt them, I am made to see what I couldn't have known, and realise that there are those who have cried out to God because of what I have done or said.

Some years ago I was crying out to the Lord because I thought he was not answering my prayers and things were not getting better. I had even fasted and things weren't better. I had done the equivalent of weeping and wailing before the Lord's altar and things were getting worse. I grew desperate and God made me see that I had really hurt someone, I had hurt him a lot. Until that happened I would have said, 'Oh, he's just too sensitive and the truth is he has hurt me a lot worse.' You couldn't have persuaded me of my guilt, but God made me see it and it was most painful.

It could be that there is someone suffering because of you. You may have hurt another person, or it was within your power to set a person free and you chose not to be gracious and do that. It may be that there are areas in your life where you think, 'God, why don't you clear my name on this?' when all the time God is telling you that you have hurt somebody, that there is somebody who has been praying about you and he is listening to his prayer and answering him instead of you. That is what Malachi is having to say. We all think of the vindication we have coming, but it is one of the hardest things in the world to recognise that we have hurt another person. What happens is that God has to roll up his sleeves to get our attention.

Behind this text is very sobering teaching. Firstly, God may wait before he decides to roll up his sleeves. And while he waits, we think everything is fine between us and God. He blesses us and speaks to us. In my own case, in the years preceding that day when God began to deal with me, I enjoyed a sense of his presence and he blessed me with insights into the things that mattered a great deal to me. Then all of a sudden I was sobered. I wondered why; I tried to work out what I had done. But it was not anything that I did that day or the day before, it was simply God's time to deal with me. He may wait before he rolls up his sleeves.

Secondly, God knows everything that is going on and he is the impartial judge. He sees things with total objectivity. He sees my hurt and he sees other people's hurt. He is the righteous judge who doesn't play favourites.

Thirdly, not only does God know everything but he forgets nothing. The Apostle Paul said that we must all stand before the judgment seat of Christ to give an account of the things done in the body, whether good or bad. Now the judgment seat of Christ has been a repetitive theme in my own ministry because my life is controlled by the knowledge that at the judgment seat, there God is going to bring to my remembrance things that I've forgotten, things that he hasn't forgotten. That is humbling.

The worst scenario is for other people to be vindicated then because of things we have done. You may say that you don't mind it happening then, but let me tell you, it is far better that it happens now. If it happens then it is going to be awful; if it happens now it is going to be painful but nothing like as bad. Saved people, those who are part of the covenant of God, are dealt with in the here and now. And it hurts. It hurts just as much as it hurt the Israelites when they flooded the Lord's altar with tears. They asked why, and Malachi told them that it was because the Lord was at work.

Fourthly, when God decides to roll up his sleeves, nothing can stop him. It could be that even as you read this book the Lord is dealing with you about certain things or relationships. Perhaps you know in your heart of hearts that you haven't been fair or have caused hurt, and you think God isn't going to pay attention to that. You don't realise how other people have been wounded. But God is listening to them while you wonder why your prayers are not being answered.

Fifthly, God does this because he loves us. And you say, 'Well, I think he loves the other person. He is coming to her rescue. He is listening to her instead of me.' Yes, but he loves you. You are the one God wants to refine, and by not answering your prayers he is getting your attention.

Malachi starts this book with the words, *'I have loved you,'* even though the people did not feel loved. And he is showing them that God wants to sort them out. My experience of God's not answering changed me, and it hurt. But he dealt with me in that way because he loved me. And far better that he deal with me now than at the judgment seat.

'During the reign of David, there was a famine of three successive years; so David sought the face of the LORD. The LORD said, "It is on account of Saul and his blood-stained house; it is because he put the Gibeonites to death"' (2 Sam. 21:1). In the book of Joshua the Gibeonites made a treaty with Israel and, like it or not, they had to be treated with respect as a result. But in the reign of King Saul that treaty was violated. You might have thought that God would have stepped in right then. He did not. It was years before he rolled up his sleeves. David was by then King. The land had three consecutive years of famine before David asked the Lord, 'Why?' And it turned out that the problem went away back to Saul's violation of that treaty. The point is that God doesn't forget.

What can we learn from this? Firstly, unconfessed sin will be either confessed or punished. And if eventually it is not confessed God will step in. He may do it on the final day or in the meantime by bringing us to our knees.

Secondly, it shows how we so easily focus on what other people have done to us and almost never on what we have done to them. Unless God rolls up his sleeves and we realise he is after us, we won't come to the point of saying,

It's not my brother or my sister, but it's me, oh, Lord,
standing in the need of prayer;
not the deacon or the preacher, but it's me, oh Lord,
standing in the need of prayer.

Thirdly, God does this because he loves us and he wants us to get sorted out. That was true of the Israelites in Malachi's day and it is true of us in ours.

Fourthly, the Lord's credibility is to be vindicated. He was a witness to all that was going on with these Israelites and a covenant was at stake, in this case a marriage covenant. It may be a different kind of covenant in your case, perhaps a promise you made to the Lord. In the Falklands War there were reports of one British soldier after another coming to Christ, the same thing in the Gulf War. They promised God they would serve him if he got them out of that mess. How many of you have done that? Have you prayed, 'God help me and I'll do what you want.' What happened then? Did God get you out of the mess and did you remember or forget your promise?

Sin unconfessed, that means sin unrepented of, remains sin in God's eyes. You may have thought the Lord doesn't notice, but he does. He sees and remembers all sin with one exception, and that is sin covered by the blood of Jesus.

11

MARRIAGE, INFIDELITY
AND DIVORCE

Has not the LORD made them one? In flesh and spirit they are his. And why one? Because he was seeking godly offspring. So guard yourself in your spirit, and do not break faith with the wife of your youth. 'I hate divorce,' says the LORD God of Israel, 'and I hate a man's covering himself with violence as with his garment,' says the LORD Almighty' (Malachi 2:15-16).

This is the order of events followed by an increasing number of couples at the present time. It is an order all too common. A man and a woman marry, then at some stage one of them is unfaithful to the other, and eventually divorce follows. In the United States one out of two marriages now ends in divorce. In the United Kingdom one in three ends in divorce, and Britain leads Europe in marriage breakdown. But this is not a new order of things; it is exactly the same as in the book of Malachi. The Israelites were married, then unfaithful, then divorced. Then they asked why the Lord paid no attention to them! *'It is because the LORD is acting as a witness between you and the wife of your youth, because you have broken faith with her, though she is your partner, the wife of your marriage covenant'* (2:14). The order that was seen in Malachi's day is being seen today; what happened then is happening now. It is a matter of history repeating itself.

I don't know if any readers might actually be contemplating divorce, but it is so common that I suspect some might. Nor do

I want to make anyone feel guilty who is divorced. But it could be that this teaching could save a marriage, and that would be wonderful. So what was happening in Israel? Divorce was widespread there, and people were using the Bible to vindicate everything they wanted to do when it came to divorce.

Whether we like it or not the Old Testament law allowed for divorce in some circumstances. But the time came when a man in ancient Israel could divorce his wife for just about any reason. If he didn't like the way she cooked his meals he could divorce her. If she lost that young look as she got older he could divorce her because of what the Scripture said. *'If a man marries a woman who becomes displeasing to him because he finds something indecent about her, and he writes her a certificate of divorce ...'* (Deut. 24:1). The word 'indecent' in the Hebrew is a vague one. It could refer to her being dishonourable to him, or it could refer to infidelity. But it also seems to be able to mean almost anything that he didn't like about her, and that is how it came to be interpreted. So he gives her a certificate of divorce. It is important that he remembers that because it affords her a little bit of protection.

The point is that the Israelites knew about that scripture and they were divorcing their wives as they lost their young looks. When they no longer looked like they would be on the cover of Vogue magazine, or its equivalent, they would say, 'It has been nice to know you but I am going to give you a certificate of divorce,' and their wives were out. Why did they do that? They did it in order to be free to marry again, and according to Malachi they were marrying non-Jewish women. Casting their eyes around they noticed that the non-Jewish women were exotic and lovely and they set their sights on marrying them.

Malachi was sent to tell them that God hates divorce even though the book of Deuteronomy written by Moses clearly allowed them to divorce. They no doubt went to Malachi and told him he was going against Scripture. How dare he tell them that God hates divorce. Didn't God write through Moses? Isn't what Moses wrote the word of God? Think of the awkwardness of Malachi's situation when he came with this message. He told them that God hated divorce and they quoted Scripture back to him. The truth is that Malachi was ahead of his time, upholding to the hilt what Jesus would say some four hundred years later. The response Malachi met with was exactly the same as met Jesus when people asked him why it was that if divorce was so bad Moses said that they could grant certificates of divorce. Jesus told them that Moses permitted them to divorce their wives because their hearts were hard, but that it was not this way from the beginning, and that when a man and woman came together they are no longer two but one, that what God had joined together man should not separate. Jesus upheld Malachi, but Malachi stood alone at the time.

Here we meet one of the most important things God has said in relation to the family: '*I hate divorce*'. Why is this so relevant? We are living in a time when some newscasters, politicians, and many people who make headlines, laugh at the family. The nuclear family, a husband, wife and children, is God's institution. God loves the family and his word teaches the sanctity and permanence of marriage. This is something Dad drummed into me, and something that we should be drumming into our children. So many things I feel strongly about and teach come from having had a strong father. I thank God I had a strong father, and I mean strong. I was often scared of him. Latterly he suffered from Alzheimer's Disease and lay in bed in a foetal position hardly knowing where he was. When I looked at him, I remembered I was once actually afraid of this man; I had so much respect for him. But I thank God for a father who used to say to me, 'Son, marriage is for life, for life.' Sometimes it made me afraid to go out with a girl for I would find myself wondering if I wanted to marry her and be with her all my life. The idea of divorce was out of the question.

And that is what Malachi is saying here. Jesus allows divorce in the case of infidelity, and the Apostle Paul adds the case of desertion. What God is saying here through Malachi is what pleases him best. Anybody thinking of marriage should look carefully at these verses. The prophet makes four points: marriage and the flesh; marriage and the family; marriage and faithfulness, and marriage and faith.

Firstly, marriage and the flesh. *'Has not the LORD made them one? In flesh and spirit they are his'* (2:15). *'For this reason a man will leave his father and mother and be united to his wife, and they will become one flesh'* (Gen. 2:24). God ordained that sexual intercourse consummates marriage; that is what makes a man and a woman one flesh. That is the biblical basis for fidelity. Anybody who sleeps with a woman becomes one flesh with her right then and there. It is not required to go to a church and get married in order to be one flesh; you don't have to go to an official to be married in order to be one flesh. Paul wrote, *'Do you not know that he who unites himself with a prostitute is one with her in body? For it is said, "The two will become one flesh"'* (1 Cor. 6:16). That is what sexual union does. You become one flesh. That is why God was angry. His people were becoming one flesh with non-Jewish women who didn't care anything about the Lord.

Secondly, marriage and the family. Malachi asks, *'Has not the LORD made them one?'* (2:15) Why did he ask that? *'In flesh and spirit they are his ... Because he was seeking godly offspring.'* There are two things at stake here. The first is that God is addressing the tribe of Judah, and he wanted Judah to be pure because he had promised that the Messiah would come through the line of Judah. If everybody in Judah began to marry non-Jewish women the lineage of Jesus Christ, who was to be born of the seed of David of the tribe of Judah, would be seriously injured. Because God did not want this to happen he wanted to keep Judah pure. The second reason is that all children of the covenant were to be godly. They were to be the 'godly offspring'. Marrying non-Jewish women militated against this. The Lord was determined to keep families pure so that those brought up in the family of God would be taught the Scriptures. Did you know that the family in ancient Israel was intended to be the school in which God's way was learned? *'Honour your father and your mother, so that you may live long in the land the LORD your God is giving you'* (Ex. 20:12). If children do not respect their parents the whole authority that God gave to the family as an institution erodes and is broken down. You should never speak in an impudent manner to your father or mother regardless of how old you or they may be. In Deuteronomy Moses said, *'Fix these words of mine in your hearts and minds; tie them as symbols on your hands and bind them on your foreheads. Teach them to your children, talking about them when you sit at home and when you walk along the road, when you lie down and when you get up'* (11:18-19).

In Malachi's day this divine institution was being threatened just as it is today. It is my belief that the only hope for Britain, America and the West at the present time, when marriage breakdown is bringing about a disintegration of the family and children grow up lacking sexual identity, is for fathers to be as strong as mine was. They would make a big difference, both as role models and through teaching. I believe that the lack of strong parenting, especially strong fathering, is one of the reasons for the ever-increasing homosexuality in the West, where it is even being taught in schools as a valid option. How that must grieve the heart of God. There is no hope for the family if this continues and the only thing that will stop it is a massive turning to Christ. Then people would be sorry for their sins and repent of them. Families would be brought together and children have a new start, and there would be a new generation. We should pray that Jesus will tarry and allow for the family to be brought back and given a place of dignity.

Thirdly, marriage and faithfulness. Only when parents remain faithful to their marriage vows can their children be given the security that provides the basis for godly living. The seventh commandment is, *'You shall not commit adultery'* (Ex. 20:14). Why do you suppose God gave the seventh commandment? There are two reasons. First, the self-esteem of the wife. What it does for the self-esteem of a wife when her husband is unfaithful to her is unthinkable. She feels rejected; she feels she is nothing, and she feels she has no value. It works the other way when a wife is unfaithful to her husband. It is so degrading. So the seventh commandment is to preserve the self-esteem of the married couple. Second, it is for the security and wellbeing of the family. That's what was disintegrating in Malachi's day and why he spoke out as he did.

The Israelites were going to the altar with tears, weeping and wailing, accusing God of not listening to them and demanding to know why. God said, I will tell you why, it is because I am acting as the witness between you and the wife of your youth with whom you have broken faith. I have got Deuteronomy 24 on my side, these men would say, I can just send her away. And God said, No. God says, *'I hate divorce.'* That shows how he really feels. But when Malachi tells them that, it sounds as though he is going against God's law. He was not the first prophet to do that. Did you ever wonder why God said through prophets like Amos or Hosea, 'I hate your sacrifices' when it was he who gave his people the sacrifices in the book of Leviticus? These prophets had their work cut out for them because it looked as though they were going against the law.

There are Christians today who believe that we ought to be still under the law. I believe that the law, which dates from the 13th century BC up to the time of Christ, is to be seen as a parenthesis in God's salvation history. Prophets like Amos and Malachi were able to see this. They saw that the sacrifices pointed to the coming Messiah who would die on a cross. And they were aware that these sacrifices that pointed beyond themselves had become ends in themselves. The good news for Christians is that all of these Old Testament sacrifices were fulfilled when Jesus died on the cross. For that reason the blood of Jesus, not of sacrifices, washes away all sin, takes away all guilt, whether you are divorced, single, homosexual, heterosexual; whether you have been a child molester or murderer. If you seek God's forgiveness the blood of Jesus will wipe it all away as though it had never happened. That is wonderful! And those prophets saw that coming.

Fourth, marriage and faith. Twice there is the expression *'guard yourself in your spirit'* (2:15, 16). This is where it begins, in your own spirit. As a husband grows older he needs to realise that integrity calls him to love the wife of his youth even though she isn't as beautiful as she used to be. Men sometimes grow more attractive as they age and they may be tempted to fancy themselves as manly. But if you want to be a real man you should love the wife of your youth. These poor women in Malachi's day were crying out because they knew they couldn't compete with the young, exotic non-Jewish women, and they said, 'Lord what am I going to do? My husband is leaving me.' Their cries were heard and God sent Malachi to warn their husbands. God's way is right. It is integrity. *'Guard yourself in your spirit,'* God still says today, do not break faith as your wife grows older and do not divorce her. That is all about sex. But Malachi's plea is to think of the children, think of the future generation.

12

WHEN BELIEVERS
QUESTION GOD

You have wearied the LORD with your words. 'How have we wearied him,' you ask. By saying, 'All who do evil are good in the eyes of the LORD, and he is pleased with them' or 'Where is the God of justice' (Malachi 2:17).

You know the feeling of making another person tired, when you see that as you talk on and on they are looking bored and they want you to stop, but you are insensitive to it until the last minute and then you are so embarrassed? None of us wants to do that to anyone. I don't want to do that with my preaching. I would always rather finish when a congregation was hoping I would go on than stop long after they wished the sermon was over. We don't want to tire people, and we don't want to tire God either. But how could we make God tired, especially as Scripture says, *'The LORD is the everlasting God, the Creator of the ends of the earth. He will not grow tired or weary, and his understanding no-one can fathom'* (Is. 40:28). According to that verse God cannot become weary, yet Malachi says that the Israelites have wearied the Lord with their words. They have made him tired.

If I made God tired by my words I would want to know about it. It is not something I would want to continue doing if I were aware of it. When Malachi told them that they made God tired, they wanted to know how they were doing it. So Malachi gives two reasons: one, by saying that all who do evil are good in the eyes of the Lord; two, by assuming that the Lord is pleased with them and by demanding to know where the God of justice is.

Firstly, Malachi does not say that we weary God by our praying. I am so glad to know that. I would hate to think that I could weary the Lord with my prayers. Jesus told his disciples, *'they should always pray and not give up* (Luke 18:1). And, as far as I am concerned, the most encouraging passage in the Bible on prayer are the verses that follow where Jesus encourages us to ask for the same thing day after day until our prayer is answered (Luke 18:3-8). If you think you weary the Lord by your praying, you do not. The devil may make you think you do but I can tell you that God is pleased when you keep coming to him.

Secondly, we do not weary the Lord by confessing our sins to him. *'If we confess our sins, he is faithful and just and will forgive us our sins and purify us from all unrighteousness'* (I John 1:8). Confessing does not just mean saying the right words in your head; it mean being truly sorry. That is a good word for all of us. If you are conscious that you have grieved the Lord, tell him, and in doing that your obedience will bring honour and glory to his name.

Thirdly, we don't weary God by pouring out our hearts even if we are complaining. *'I cry aloud to the LORD; I lift up my voice to the LORD for mercy. I pour out my complaint before him; before him I tell my trouble'* (Ps. 142:1-2). That does not weary the Lord. If you have complaints, tell him. If you have troubles, tell him. If you are hurt, tell him. If you are disappointed, tell him. He does not get tired of that.

You may think that was exactly what the Israelites were doing, they were complaining to the Lord. They were, but they crossed over a line that should never be crossed. It is when we cross over that line that we make God tired. Their complaint was that evil was being approved by God because he was blessing evil people. That was sarcasm borne out of anger. They said, 'God obviously isn't against evil. Look at all these evil people who are being blessed.' They had crossed over a line. We have all had those thoughts, even the godly, which is why Psalm 37 starts as it does. *'Do not fret because of evil men or be envious of those who do wrong; for like the grass they will soon wither, like green plants they will soon die away'* (v. 1-2). Why did David say that? It is because we have all seen evil men thriving. They don't get caught and they seem to make more money. They get away with crimes; they get away with everything that you know is wrong. But God doesn't cut them down, and that makes us think and question.

The whole of the book of Habakkuk is on this subject. *'Why do you make me look at injustice? Why do you tolerate wrong?'* (Hab. 1:3). All believers have asked questions like that. But the people in Malachi's day were doing more than that; they were claiming that evil was approved by God because evildoers appeared to be blessed. They crossed over the line by saying that there is no God of justice. They should not have said that. They underestimated the effect such words would have on God.

Often we don't take our words seriously enough. I have this problem. All my life I have wondered why anyone should listen to me. Some may think I have a great self-image and am full of self-confidence, but they are wrong because I have a real inferiority complex. I am amazed when people see me as an authoritative figure and think my word is worth listening to because I know I am utterly unworthy to be in a pulpit. But the position I am in makes me realise that I have to watch what I say because people are listening to me. God is also listening. And when we say things that lay at his feet the charge that he approves of evil because evil men are being blessed, he hears that, and he doesn't like it.

Who were these men who were saying that? They were Jews who felt God didn't love them. The first thing Malachi did was tell them that they were loved. Their response was, 'Prove it.

We don't feel loved.' He then had to tell them that they hadn't shown love to God, and that when you don't show love to God, and you aren't doing what you ought to be doing, it is not surprising that you don't feel loved. The truth is that although God loved them their complaints were, at worst, bordering on questioning his very existence and, at best, trying to manipulate him into feeling sorry for them. When the temple had been rebuilt many years before, and God hadn't come in the miraculous way they thought he would come, the people felt he had let them down. They went too far in their complaints then and they were doing the same now. Why is this important to us? I think there are three reasons. Firstly, questioning God is nothing new. Malachi was written about 2,400 years ago, and we find people still questioning God today.

Secondly, the questions people raise today are not new. We've all heard people ask how a God of love could allow suffering. That is the most common complaint we get. I went out on the streets speaking to people on Saturdays for nearly twenty years and, when I got someone to stand and talk, nine times out of ten that was their question. They thought they were coming up with something new, that no-one had thought of it before. The questions, 'If God is all-powerful and all-loving why doesn't he stop evil and trouble?' and 'Why does he allow this to happen to me?' must be among the most common questions in the world. You don't have to be highly educated to ask these questions, they come naturally. And the Israelites were asking these questions, these very questions, 2,400 years ago. Thirdly, the covenant people of God raised these questions, not just those outside the family. It is one thing to fret because of evil people who seem to prosper. Habakkuk asked, *Why do you tolerate wrong?*' (Hab. 1:3). That is a legitimate question. But there is such a thing as going too far, and that is when you make God tired.

What is the line that we must not cross over? I think it is made up of four things. Firstly, when our questions become accusations; when we accuse God. It is one thing to ask why, it is quite another to point the finger and say, 'How dare you!' God does not tire of our questions and our thoughts but he will not tolerate accusations. The Psalmist said, *'I envied the arrogant when I saw the prosperity of the wicked. They have no struggles; their bodies are healthy and strong. They are free from the burdens common to man; they are not plagued by human ills'* (Ps. 73:3-5). Then he goes on and lists his complaints, questioning how can this be. Later he even found himself questioning for a moment if he had kept his heart pure in vain. Christians have asked questions like that. Perhaps you have resisted temptation, you have not given in to something, and you find yourself thinking of the opportunity you lost. You see trouble in the world and arrogant people seeming to be blessed and getting away with things. Perhaps you feel like the Psalmist that in vain you have kept your heart pure and washed your hands in innocence. But then the psalmist going on to say, *'When I tried to understand all this, it was oppressive to me till I entered the sanctuary of God; then I understood their final destiny'* (Ps. 73:16-17).

The psalmist asked questions but he did not go over the line and begin to accuse God. He did not point his finger at God. Don't ever point the finger at God. Don't do it. I would rather play with electricity with wet fingers than point at God. When we do that we don't know what we are talking about, we haven't a clue what we are doing. An all-wise God looks down on such accusations and the accusers make him tired. Isaiah 55 says, *'"For my thoughts are not your thoughts, neither are your ways my ways," declares the LORD. "As the heavens are higher than the earth, so are my ways higher than your ways and my thoughts than your thoughts"'* (v. 8-9).

Secondly, when complaining becomes cynicism. David cried aloud to the Lord and he heard. When was the last time you prayed like that? Most of our praying is under control; we don't lose control and our emotions are intact. We hold our feelings inside ourselves and pray very quietly and calmly. But imagine crying aloud. 'O God, help me! Help me!' The psalmist said, *'I cry aloud to the LORD; I lift up my voice to the LORD for mercy. I pour out my complaint before him; before him I tell my trouble'* (Ps. 142:1-2). It is all right to do that, but when complaining becomes cynicism it makes him tired. The word cynicism implies wrong motives. And being cynical about God's dealings is charging him with wrong motives. Don't ever do that. Complain to the Lord, but never become cynical.

Thirdly, when feeling let down becomes unbelief. We have all felt let down. I have referred to it elsewhere as 'the betrayal barrier.' By that I mean feeling that God has betrayed me; he has let me down. We have an example of that in Hannah. *'In bitterness of soul Hannah wept much and prayed to the LORD'* (I Sam. 1:10). Hannah was bitter but she prayed; she felt let down but she didn't give in to unbelief. If I felt let down I would pray more than ever. Twice in the Bible God says if we seek him with all our heart we will find him. Some of you may have been waiting for a breakthrough from God. You say, 'He doesn't seem to speak to me as he used to do and I don't feel his presence as I once did. I once had joy but I don't have it now. I once could talk to God and enjoy an intimacy I no longer have.' If that's the case I urge you to pray more than ever. The reason you haven't found him real may be that, in a time when God has tested you, you have given up and become cynical instead of seeking him night and day. You may even have questioned God's very existence. That is what the Israelites did.

Fourthly, when self-pity becomes anger toward God. We all know what it is to be sorry for ourselves and we know it doesn't get us anywhere. But we should never let our self-pity become anger toward God. *'Man's anger does not bring about the righteous life God desires'* (Jam. 1:20). The Greek literally means the wrath/anger of man doesn't work the righteousness of God, that is, you can't twist his arm by getting angry at him. You can't sulk and expect God to say, 'Oh I'm sorry.' When you start to sulk, God goes in the other direction. Sulking with God just doesn't work. When self-pity becomes anger towards God it makes him tired, it wearies him. The people in Malachi's day had crossed over the line. It is interesting to note that never once does God apologise to them and say, 'Oh well, let me explain. It was for this reason and that,' rather he promises them judgment.

For those who resist cynicism there will be joy and relief, and there will also be great relief for those cynics who repent. Jesus died for your cynicism, for your unbelief. Jesus died for the sin of accusing God and implying wrong motives. Jesus died for the sin of pointing the finger at him. Those sins are paid for by the blood that he shed, but they need to be confessed and rejected.

13

PRAYER SUDDENLY ANSWERED

'See, I will send my messenger, who will prepare the way before me. Then suddenly the Lord you are seeking will come to his temple; the messenger of the covenant, whom you desire, will come,' says the Lord Almighty' (Malachi 3:1).

I just love this verse and I connect it to revival. It encourages me to look for the manifestation of God's glory that I believe will come suddenly. We cannot be selective, telling the Lord that we will let him come as long as he comes in such a way as will not cost us anything, or embarrass our friends, or knock us out of our comfort zone. We cannot make God's choices. He comes as and when he chooses. Preparation is different; it can be gradual. It appears that preparation had to take place before the Lord would come suddenly. *'I will send my messenger, who will prepare the way before me'* (3:1). Preparations were also made for the Spirit's coming at Pentecost. *'When the day of Pentecost came, they were all together in one place. Suddenly a sound like the blowing of a violent wind came from heaven and filled the whole house where they were sitting'* (Acts 2:1).

At Pentecost the Lord came suddenly in a way for which there was no precedent. You can imagine all the Jewish Rabbis saying, 'Let's see if that's in the Scriptures, if there is any precedent for this.' Peter stood up and told them that what they had seen was what Joel prophesied. That did not convince them because what they saw was so altogether different. Yet there had

87

been preparation: Jesus' three years of teaching and the disciples' ten days of prayer. When the Spirit came, however, he came suddenly. Malachi says, *'Suddenly the Lord you are seeking will come to his temple'* (3:1). His coming was an answer to prayer. They were seeking the Lord.

What is this verse teaching? This is almost certainly a play on words, certainly in the Hebrew. Malachi 1:1 says, *'An oracle: The word of the LORD to Israel through Malachi.'* Malachi means 'my messenger'. Then in 3:1 we have, *'See, I will send my messenger.'* Perhaps Malachi sees himself in this role; certainly he was delivering the oracle of the Lord. The verse seems to teach that the coming of the Lord would be preceded by preparation, as though without preparation it couldn't happen. This is partly because it would show a lack of dignity. Preparations are made well in advance for a royal procession. So the coming of the Lord would be heralded by a forerunner. Isaiah says, *'A voice of one calling: "In the desert prepare the way for the LORD; make straight in the wilderness a highway for our God"'* (40:3). But although preparation was to be made, Malachi makes it clear that his coming would nonetheless be unexpected; it would be sudden.

There is a paradox here. The paradox is that without preparation there would be no coming of the Lord, while at the same time there was to be no advance notice of the time of his coming. Isaiah may have felt foolish prophesying the coming of Messiah because if people were to ask when, he would have to tell them that he did not know when he would come.

So it is with the Second Coming of the Lord. Jesus said that we would know neither the day nor the hour; that only the Father in heaven knows these things. The same was true of the coming of the Spirit at Pentecost. There was no hint when it would be. In the event the disciples prayed for ten days, but they didn't know whether it would be twenty days or a hundred days. There was, therefore, preparation with no advance notice as to time scale. This seems to be how God works. Malachi said, *'Then suddenly the Lord you are seeking will come,'* not when the Lord would come. We learn from this verse that his coming was a result of seeking but, when the prayer for his coming was answered, it was answered suddenly. The Lord's coming was answered prayer.

Why is this so important? Despite the fact that the people Malachi was addressing did not love God as they should, they still sought him. *'Suddenly the Lord you are seeking ...'* You would not have known they were seeking the Lord from what he had said to them previously. Their faith was defective; they had shown no respect for God in their sacrifices, and we could list a dozen things about them that were absolutely wrong. Yet despite all that, Malachi admits that they were seeking the Lord and that they did desire him, *'The messenger of the covenant, whom you desire, will come'* (3:1). Although these people were not loving God as they should, and not honouring God as they should, they weren't all bad. Isaiah said of Jesus, *'A bruised reed he will not break, and a smouldering wick he will not snuff out'* (Is. 42:3) and that was how God dealt with those Israelites.

Perhaps you know you are not what you ought to be and there are things in your life that you are embarrassed about, but still you would love the Lord to return and you want to be on his side when he does. Are you a 'bruised reed', are you hurting? The Lord will love you just as you are. Self-righteous Christians might stand in judgment over you. They might say you are not worthy; you are not what you ought to be. But Jesus always sees the diamond in the rough. He recognises the bruised reed and sees the smouldering wick. He sees the smoke, and where there is smoke there has got to be fire, and he commits himself to stay with that person.

The coming of the Lord would be too awesome without some preparation. That is why John the Baptist came first and then Jesus. Malachi talks of two messengers. *'I will send my messenger, who will prepare the way for me. Then suddenly the Lord you are seeking will come to his temple; the messenger of the covenant, whom you desire, will come'* (3:1) The second messenger is called the messenger of the covenant. The first messenger is John the Baptist and the second messenger is Jesus himself. For Jesus to come suddenly without there being some preparation would have been casting pearls before swine; the people would not have coped. They needed to be spoon-fed, and there are many like that today.

What does the expression 'messenger of the covenant' mean? Ancient Hebrews were familiar with covenants, agreements between two parties based upon a condition. A covenant was always sealed with blood. And this is Malachi's way of saying that the second messenger, the messenger of the covenant, would seal the covenant with his blood, the blood that dripped from Jesus as he hung on the cross. God saw that blood and swore that all who trust in Jesus' shed blood will not come under condemnation. The good news is that it doesn't matter what list of sins you bring with you, you can do what other people are too righteous to do, namely flee to the cross. If Adolf Hitler had asked for mercy five minutes before he died he would have been saved. While self-righteous Lutherans all over Germany would not bother to trust what Jesus had done for them on the cross, Adolf Hitler could have received a free pardon.

This verse also shows the importance of being ready for answered prayer. 400 years after Malachi, a man named Zechariah was burning incense in the temple. Suddenly, the angel Gabriel appeared and scared Zechariah nearly out of his mind. Imagine the conversation that might have taken place. Gabriel said, 'Relax, don't be afraid. Your prayer has been heard.' 'Good,' said Zechariah, 'Oh, by the way, what prayer?' 'Elizabeth and you prayed for a son,' reminded Gabriel. 'That prayer? That was about twenty-five years ago. You have made a mistake you know, Elizabeth is far to old to have babies.' 'Oh,' says Gabriel,

'I have been given orders from heaven to tell you that Elizabeth will conceive and bear a son.' Zechariah wasn't ready and he foolishly didn't believe the angel. 'By the way, I am sorry I have to do this, Zechariah,' Gabriel said, 'but before I go back to heaven you are going to be struck dumb and you will not be able to speak till the baby comes' (see Luke 1:8-25).

Zechariah was not ready for answered prayer. Any prayer prayed in the will of God will be answered. John said, *'If we ask anything according to his will, he hears us'* (1 John 5:14). We don't always know we are praying in God's will. He doesn't always tell us if we are. Zechariah and Elizabeth got it right when they asked for a son but it was many years before their son was born. Then when his prayer was answered Zechariah didn't believe it.

There are two principles involved here. Principle number one, any prayer prayed in the will of God will be answered. Principle number two, the shape answered prayer takes is determined by our readiness at the time. Zechariah wasn't ready and he was struck dumb, but his prayer was still answered. What ought to have been his finest hour caught him blushing. You can imagine people from all over the Judean desert and hillsides going up to Zechariah and Elizabeth and saying, 'Zechariah we are so happy for you. We are so pleased Elizabeth is going to have a baby and we have come by to congratulate you both.' But Zechariah can't speak; he is struck dumb. His prayer was answered, but the shape the answer took was determined by his unreadiness. How much more important it is to be ready when we don't know when Jesus is coming.

There are three final points: preparation, prolonging and promise. Firstly, preparation. How do you prepare? You seek the Lord; that means praying. You spend time with him. It doesn't matter how you do it, but you talk to him. Back in the autumn of 1955 I began to think that if God didn't come to my rescue I couldn't go on. And I began to pray, 'Lord, come. Lord, please come. Jesus, come.' I was a student at Trevecca Nazarene College at the time, and I decided that I would use every minute I had to pray. I got up as early as I could and did nothing but pray until breakfast. Then I went to class and if I had free time between eleven and twelve I went back and got on my knees in the dormitory. No-one was there and I would pray for an hour before I went for lunch. Right after lunch I went back again and prayed until I had to go to another class. When that class was over I'd go back and pray. I did that for weeks then, on 31st October 1955, even though I was not prepared, the Lord came. I have never been the same since. *'Suddenly the Lord you are seeking will come'* (3:1).

We need to pray, pray, pray. We wonder why the church is powerless; it is because it doesn't pray. These words are from Martin Luther's journal, 'I have a very busy day today. Must spend not two hours but three in prayer today.' He reckoned the more he prayed, the more time he would have to do things. If the Lord suddenly comes will you be embarrassed because you are not prepared?

Secondly, prolonging. That means you have to wait longer than you thought you would. The temple the Israelites went to was the second one since the Babylonian captivity. They had expected the Lord to come generations ago. That's why Malachi assures them that it is still going to happen, he is going to come, and when he comes he will come suddenly. The time can be prolonged, but he will come. What thrills me is that Jesus could come any minute. He could come before you finish reading this chapter.

Thirdly, the promise. *'Do not throw away your confidence; it will be richly rewarded. You need to persevere so that when you have done the will of God, you will receive what he has promised'* (Heb. 10:35). If your life isn't what it ought to be when the Lord appears you are going to be blushing; you will be embarrassed and very sorry. You say, 'What if I get everything in order and the Lord doesn't come?' If you do that you are better off anyway.

While we wait we can worship; while we wait we can walk in the light, we can praise him, we can honour him with a holy life. Even if revival doesn't come in my lifetime I'll serve him to the end.

14

DO WE WANT REVIVAL
AFTER ALL?

*'See, I will send my messenger, who will prepare the way before me.
Then suddenly the Lord you are seeking will come to his temple; the
messenger of the covenant, whom you desire, will come,' says the
Lord Almighty. But who can endure the day of his coming? Who can
stand when he appears? For he will be like a refiner's fire or a launderer's
soap. He will sit as a refiner and purifier of silver; he will purify the
Levites and refine them like gold and silver. Then the LORD will have
men who will bring offerings in righteousness'* (Malachi 3:1-3).

Do we really want revival? Nearly all my life I have wanted to
see revival. I am not sure when I first had an appetite for it, but
I grew up in what was something of a revival atmosphere. I was
brought up in the tail end of revivals that started in the previous
century in Cane Ridge in Kentucky. Consequently, I have longed
for revival, and prayed for it, through all my ministries. In 1985,
I introduced the first prayer covenant in Westminster Chapel.
There were several petitions and one of them was a prayer for
true revival in the congregation. After five years we closed that
covenant but revived the idea some years later. Then, instead of
praying for true revival in Westminster Chapel, we prayed for
the manifestation of God's glory in our midst along with an
ever-increasing openness in us to the manner in which he chose
to appear.

The people in Malachi's day prayed the equivalent of that

prayer. Perhaps that comes as a surprise when we realise their many imperfections. While there were gross imperfections Malachi affirms them on one thing, that some of them were seeking the Lord. Some still longed for God to come.

Malachi tells them how their prayer will be answered, and I don't think it is exactly what they had in mind. I believe what they imagined was that God would affirm them against their enemies in the world. Israel had a great history and the people knew it through their oral tradition. What they wanted was for God to come in the way he had done in the great days of Solomon, when the temple was filled with his glory and all the nations stood in awe of Israel. They were looking not only for the honour of God's name to be restored, but the honour of Israel to be seen in the world. That is what they wanted, and they sincerely believed that when God came that was how it would be. But things were to turn out very differently. That was why I reworded our prayer covenant when we revived it, and began praying for the manifestation of God's glory.

What is the difference? The difference is that praying for revival was, in a sense, setting a limit on God, and that is what these Israelites were doing. Praying for the manifestation of God's glory is not dictating to him what he should do. Why did we use the word 'glory'? The word glory is the nearest we can get to the essence of God. If we only had one word to describe the God of the Bible, that word would have to be glory. He is a God of glory. We prayed that he would manifest his glory and we did not tell him how to do it. What is revival? Revival is certainly one manifestation of God's glory. Praying for such a revival is inviting God to be himself. But we must not limit him, and that was the Israelites' mistake.

What does this teach us? Firstly, when the preparation is complete the Lord will suddenly come into his temple. That is what is implied in 3:1. *'See, I will send my messenger, who will prepare the way before me. Then suddenly the Lord you are seeking will come to his temple ...'* I wonder how many of you are consciously aware of being prepared. Speaking personally, God has been dealing with me for a number of years and what he has shown me about myself has not been pretty. Often, when he has shown me painful things, I have asked him why he didn't show me them before. If I had known them earlier I could have been a better husband, a better dad and a better minister. I believe this is part of being prepared. God is preparing me as he shows me more and more things I need to confess and learn. Surely I'm not alone in that experience; we are all in it together.

Secondly, this passage is teaching that his coming would be different from what was expected. The people expected Israel to be put back on the map and their former days of glory to return. But what Malachi tells them is that when the Lord comes into the temple it would be to do two things: to convince and convict of sin, and to cleanse. Jesus said, *'Unless I go away, the Counsellor will not come to you; but if I go, I will send him to you. When he comes, he will convict the world of guilt in regard to sin and righteousness and judgment'* (John 16:7-8). The primary work of the Spirit is to reprove the world of sin. The unrepentant, the unforgiven, will not go to heaven. They need to realise they are sinners in need of a Saviour. They need to know they have offended God. When the Spirit grips you – and only he can do it – you realise you have offended God, and that can be a very frightening ordeal. I knew one lady who told me that when she was first aware of her sin she thought she was losing her mind.

Thirdly, Malachi teaches the need for cleansing from sin. God doesn't convict us of our sin just to make us feel miserable when we become aware that we have offended him. This is why he sent his Son into the world to die on a cross. Jesus took our sins upon himself; he paid for our sins by his own blood. Therefore, when we acknowledge our sin and look to Jesus to be saved, God gives us a free pardon. We go from being miserable sinners to being cleansed and exhilarated. That is the process.

'Who can endure the day of his coming? Who can stand when he appears? ... He will sit as a refiner and purifier of silver; he will purify the Levites and refine them like gold and silver' (vs. 2-3). We should think twice before we pray for revival or the manifestation of his glory. I wonder if God looks down from heaven and hears our prayer and says, 'Do they know what they are asking for?' And are we willing for him to come as he chooses. Remember, he will sit as a refiner and a purifier of hearts and lives.

Three final points from the verse. Firstly, Malachi is giving the people an advance warning of how it is going to be. He tells them that when their preparation is complete the Lord will come into his temple. Then he says, 'Are you ready for this? Who can stand it? The Lord will appear, yes, but this is how it will be.' Peter says, 'For it is time for judgment to begin with the family of God; and if it begins with us, what will the outcome be for those who do not obey the gospel of God? And, "If it is hard for the righteous to be saved, what will become of the ungodly and the sinner?"' (1 Pet. 4:17-18). It is going to be bad enough for anybody who is a part of the church because judgment begins at the house of God, but what will it be like for those who are not saved? What in your life do you suspect would have to change if God were to come suddenly in revival today? And if you already know what would have to change then why not change it now.

Secondly, this is an announcement of wrath. Why is God angry? He is angry because he is a holy God. He doesn't like it when those who are bought with the blood of Jesus try to see how close they can get to the world and still be all right. 'Friendship with the world is hatred towards God' (Jam. 4:4). If your lifestyle allows you to do things that you know do not bring glory to God's name, you need to live differently. If you allow yourself to be engrossed in things that you have a shrewd suspicion would disgrace you if God came in power, and you felt his power and holiness, then stop them now.

Thirdly, his is awesome wonder. *'Who can endure the day of his coming? Who can stand when he appears?'* (3:2) shows how real God is. When Jesus comes in reviving power everybody is going to say. 'Hey this is real! All that we have been preaching is true.' And it is. There is Jesus and he is the son of God. He died on the cross, was raised from the dead and is coming again. These are facts. When he comes, people are going to be shaken rigid.

For years I spent my Saturdays on the streets of London talking to passers-by. They would talk about heaven and hell without being the slightest bit bothered because they didn't really believe they exist. If you put them under a lie detector you would discover they don't believe there is a God; they don't believe the Bible, and they don't believe Jesus was raised from the dead. They are not bothered. Can you imagine what it would be like for them in revival?

When that time comes, the first thing that will happen is that the church will be awakened. Jesus told of a marriage. All the preparations were made and the bridegroom was awaited. *'At midnight the cry rang out: "Here's the bridegroom! Come out to meet him!" Then all the virgins woke up and trimmed their lamps. The foolish ones said to the wise, "Give us some of your oil; our lamps are going out." "No," they replied … But while they* (the foolish virgins) *were on their way to buy the oil, the bridegroom arrived'* (Matt. 25:6-10). Jesus' story describes those who are part of the church who, when revival comes, realise they have been asleep. Three things characterise sleep. You don't know you are asleep until you wake up. When you are asleep you do things in your dreams that you wouldn't do when you were wide awake. And you hate the sound of an alarm. Then when you wake up you can't believe you let yourself sleep.

There are times when I have been like that, when I have

allowed things to come into my life that ought not to have been there. Yet how loving God is. He speaks through Malachi to people in that condition; he uses the prophet to get their attention. That shows God loves them and us. What God wants for us is what is best for us.

Do we want revival after all? I believe I do. It will be as though the Second Coming was brought forward to give us a taste of what it will be like when the Lord comes in glory. It will also be judgment brought forward, an advance warning of what it will be like on the Judgment Day.

15

JUDGMENT IN GOD'S HOUSE

'See, I will send my messenger, who will prepare the way before me. Then suddenly the Lord you are seeking will come to his temple; the messenger of the covenant, whom you desire, will come,' says the Lord Almighty. But who can endure the day of his coming? Who can stand when he appears? For he will be like a refiner's fire or a launderer's soap. He will sit as a refiner and purifier of silver; he will purify the Levites and refine them like gold and silver. Then the LORD will have men who will bring offerings in righteousness, and the offerings of Judah and Jerusalem will be acceptable to the LORD, as in days gone by, as in former years. So I will come near to you for judgment. I will be QUICK to testify against sorcerers, adulterers and perjurers, against those who defraud labourers of their wages, who oppress the widows and the fatherless, and deprive aliens of justice, but do not fear me,' says the LORD Almighty" (Malachi 3:1-5).

The Bible says that judgment begins at the house of God, first with the leadership then with the people. If that's the case where will the sinner and the ungodly appear? Would you be pleased if the Lord decided to come and judge us and sort us out right now? If that were how he chose to come would you still want him? I would, because if I am not right with him I want to know it. If there is anything in my life that is not pleasing him I want to know about it. I want to know any area of rebellion and any area in which I am not walking in the light. *"'The Lord you are seeking will come to his temple; the messenger of the covenant, whom you desire, will come," says the Lord Almighty'* (3:1).

People wanted the Lord to come, and God is going to come, says Malachi, but he goes on to ask, *'Who can endure the day of his coming? Who can stand when he appears?'* (3:2) What they wanted was for God to come and restore Israel to its former glory, taking them back to the days of Solomon when the temple in all its magnificence let the world know that Israel was special. All of that had changed, but they expected that at the Lord's coming Israel would once again be vindicated. I wonder how much our desire for revival could be just as phoney, just as false. The only way we can know for sure that our desire for revival is true is to invite God to come any way he chooses. Let it not be said that the reason we want him to come is for the pride and glory of our churches. The great error of ancient Israel was that the people always wanted God to come in a way that suited their taste. That is precisely why Israel missed Messiah 2,000 years ago. Shakespeare said, 'To thy own self be true.' When God comes he will be true to himself.

The Israelites, who were trying to get away with wrong living and substandard sacrifices, expected God to come to his temple and turn a blind eye to it all. Malachi says, 'That's not on.' The Levites, the priests, were going right against God's law and still saying, 'Lord, come.' The Lord says, I am going to come, but I am going to have something to say about what you are doing and how you are living. Malachi says, *'Who can endure the day of his coming? Who can stand when he appears?'*

Revival can be seen as being heaven and/or the judgment brought forward. Why might revival be heaven brought forward? In revival there is a great sense of God's presence and great joy, both of these will be found in heaven. Many people are healed, and there will be no sickness in heaven. There will be no pain in heaven, no broken hearts and no broken marriages. Heaven brought forward changes lives, brings families together and takes dope addicts off the streets. Not only is revival heaven brought forward but it is also judgment brought forward. One day we are going to have to give an account of our lives, and when God comes in great reviving power it will be a foretaste of that judgement day. If that were how he came we would feel naked and exposed and we would think that everybody could see what was going on in our hearts even though it would be happening privately. God would make us aware of things in our lives and deal with them. How could God appear and not deal with sin? That is why Malachi said he would be like a refiner's fire or a launderer's soap.

What is launderer's soap? It is what makes dirty clothes clean. This is a type of what Jesus did for us on the cross. Because Jesus died on the cross bearing all the dirt of our sin we are promised that all our sins are forgiven, washed away, and we are given the robe of the righteousness of Christ. He makes us clean and he gives us a new beginning. Refiner's fire removes impurities from precious metals. This is a type of sanctification because God wants our appearance to glorify him, he wants our substance to glorify him. God cares about the honour of his name. He is honoured by the outward lives of his people, but equally he, who knows all our thoughts, wants us to be right in ourselves. That honours him too.

When the Lord comes, he will begin his judgement with the priests and the Levites and then turn to everyone else. Here we have a principle regarding the order of the judgment. It is the same pattern that Peter describes. *'It is time for judgment to begin with the family of God; and if it begins with us, what will the outcome be for those who do not obey the gospel of God?'* (I Pet. 4:17).

'He will sit as a refiner and purifier of silver; he will purify the Levites and refine them like gold and silver' (3:3). First God will purify the Levites. In ancient times you knew that gold or silver was refined because you could use it as a mirror. That's how pure God expected the Levites to be. Then God will purify the priests, the equivalent of the ministry. *'Not many of you*

should presume to be teachers, my brothers, because you know that we who teach will be judged more strictly' (Jas. 3:1). Why does God judge the leadership more strictly? It is because that to whom much is given, from them much shall be required. This is one of the reasons Spurgeon used to tell people who weren't sure whether they were called to the ministry, that if they could do anything else they should do it.

There are people in the ministry today whom God didn't call to be there. They went into the ministry for wrong reasons. And there are some who badly want to be ministers even though they are successful at doing other things. I tell them that if they succeed at other things that's a pretty strong hint that they are not called to the ministry. If you are called into the ministry you can't do anything else but preach. If you try to do other things you often fail at them until you realise that God is, as it were, giving you no alternatives. It could be that when God comes in reviving power that all of us who are leaders will see things that we haven't seen before, and we'll welcome him for showing them to us.

After judging the Levites and priests, God will judge his people generally. *'Then the LORD will have men who will bring offerings in righteousness, and the offerings of Judah and Jerusalem will be acceptable to the LORD, as in days gone by, as in former years'* (3:3-4). 'As in days gone by' is an interesting phrase, and when the people heard it they probably thought of Moses, David and Solomon. In other words, they wanted it like it used to be. But God says that there are things that have to be put right first. And it may well be that we too have some historical consciousness. We want things to be as they were in Luther's day, or Calvin's day, or in the days of Jonathan Edwards. Wouldn't it be wonderful if that were to happen?

The judgment does not end with the family of God because it goes from his people to those who are not. If I were not a Christian I would be scared to death at this thought, for if judgment begins *'with us, what will the outcome be for those who do not obey the gospel of God? And, "If it is hard for the righteous to be saved, what will become of the ungodly and the sinner?"'* (I Pet. 4:17-18). If you stood before God today and he asked why he should let you into heaven, what would you say? Are you ready if God comes in judgment?

Malachi lists three categories of sin. Firstly, there is what I call satanic sin. You may say that all sin is satanic, and in a sense that is true, but there is a certain type of sin that is almost devoted to Satan himself, in which people give themselves to him. That is why God says, *'I will come near to you for judgment. I will be quick to testify against sorcerers'* (3:5). Satanic sin involves the occult; it wants to go outside the true God for some kind of secret knowledge of the future. If you give yourself over to something that is not of the Holy Spirit, so that you might have secret access to what is going to happen to you, you let yourself into something occultish, something devilish. If you have any involvement in things like ouija boards, good luck charms or astrology charts, stop them immediately! If you have books that pertain to astrology, or anything else that has to do with the occult, destroy them right away. All these allow the devil to get in. That is why I call involvement in the occult satanic sin.

Secondly, there is sexual sin. *'I will be quick to testify against ... adulterers'* (3:5). Sexual sin is often the main impediment to coming to Christ. People don't want to give up their current sex life and they know that the Bible says that sex is to be contained within the bonds of marriage. I realise that there are those who are lonely and my heart goes out to them; Jesus' heart did too, but God instituted the family for the purpose of bringing up children in security, and sexual sin comes in the way of that. Children born out of wedlock are brought up without that security and without a good father image. And a society that moves away from God's ideal of the family eventually goes awry. Look at what is happening today.

Thirdly, there is social sin. *"'I will be quick to testify against ... perjurers, against those who defraud labourers of their wages, who oppress the widows and the fatherless, and deprive aliens of justice, but do not fear me," says the LORD Almighty'* (3:5). In the Epistle of James we have a situation where Christians who worked for Christians were dealt with unfairly. *'The wages you failed to pay the workmen who mowed your fields are crying out against you ...'* (Jas. 5:4). I hate to say it, but working for a Christian is not always wonderful. I wish that were not the case, but it is, because even the best of Christians are not perfect. The situation James wrote about was exactly the same as in Malachi's day.

Before we condemn these employers we have to ask ourselves if we owe anyone money. It is dishonouring to God not to pay our debts, and the withholding of wages is unthinkable. James says, *'The cries of the harvesters have reached the ears of the Lord Almighty* (Jas. 5:4). Those unpaid Christians thought no-one was listening to them, their employer certainly was not, but their cries were heard by God. If you have been hurt by a fellow-Christian God knows all about it. And if you are an unfair employer, or you are hurting your fellow believers, there will be a pay-day some day. If there are things in your life that you know God is going to expose then don't wait till he does it, put them right now.

Malachi goes on to say that there are people *'who oppress the widows and the fatherless'* (3:5). There was a feeling that widows and the fatherless were not important people. You wouldn't want to oppress somebody who had a little bit of stature and prestige but if it is a widow who can't defend herself you can get away with it, and the same with the fatherless. But you cannot get away with it because God knows. Could it be that blessing is withheld from some churches because their members are committing social sins?

Malachi continues, *'I will be quick to testify ... against ... those who ... deprive aliens of justice, but do not fear me'* (3:5).

It is not a nice feeling being an alien, I remember what I felt like when I first moved to England. Sometimes even Christians are against you because you are not like them; you are foreign. God says he will testify against people who discriminate against aliens, who make them feel different, who make them feel unwelcome. Those who behave in that way can only do so because they do not fear the Lord. That is why Malachi adds the phrase, '*but do not fear me*,' at the end of the list of people to be judged. If you know that there is something for which you deserve judgment, do something about it now, don't wait until the Lord comes in revival or in glory. Think how ashamed and embarrassed you will be otherwise.

16

THE UNCHANGING GOD

'I the LORD do not change. So you, O descendants of Jacob, are not destroyed. Ever since the time of your forefathers you have turned away from my decrees and have not kept them. Return to me, and I will return to you,' says the LORD Almighty. But you ask, 'How are we to return?' (Malachi 3:6-7).

Here there is a tremendous word for backsliders who think that God does not love them, who feel that if they were to die at this moment they would be lost eternally. Malachi addresses people like that. He tells them that the God who loved them when they first came to him in faith has not stopped loving them. Nothing has changed.

My first sermon was preached when I was at Trevecca Nazarene College, in Nashville, Tennessee, and this is how it came about. As I was walking on the campus with a friend, I told him I felt called to preach and that my church was giving me a licence to preach. The professor of Greek, who overheard the conversation, said, 'You will preach your first sermon in my church on Wednesday night.' I had two days notice, and I almost panicked. I probably did panic. I preached on, *'Great is thy faithfulness'* (Lam. 3:23). I have looked at that verse in a very special way ever since, knowing how I leaned on it for my very first sermon.

That verse connects with this one. God's faithfulness is great because he does not change, and it does not change. Also in that sermon I quoted James 1:17, *'Every good and perfect gift is from above, coming down from the Father of the heavenly lights, who does not change like shifting shadows,'* or *'in whom there is no variableness neither shadow of turning'* (AV). Other verses say much the same thing. *'God is not a man, that he should lie, nor a son of man, that he should change his mind'* (Num. 23:19). *'He who is the Glory of Israel does not lie or change his mind; for he is not a man, that he should change his mind* (1 Sam. 15:29).

There are passages in Scripture that say God does change his mind. For example, Jonah marched into Nineveh with God's warning that in forty days the city would be overthrown. The news spread like wildfire, even reaching the king of Nineveh who urged everybody to pray and fast. The king hoped that God would relent and with compassion turn from his fierce anger. And he did. *'When God saw what they did and how they turned from their evil ways, he had compassion and did not bring upon them the destruction he had threatened'* (Jon. 3:10). Again, when Isaiah went to King Hezekiah and told him to get his house in order because he was going to die, Hezekiah turned his face to the wall and pleaded with the Lord. When Isaiah came back, he told the King that the Lord had heard his cry and seen his tears and added fifteen years to his life. God changed his mind. A third example was when God, through Elijah, warned King Ahab and gave him no hope, Ahab repented in dust and ashes. Then God postponed what he was going to do. These passages seem to show God changing his mind. But in every situation where that happened it was a case of people, who had been warned by God, pleading with him and praying that he would have mercy. God was not changing his mind; he was using his word to stir them up to pray so that he could do what he wanted to do anyway. God has a way of driving us to our knees to seek his face in order that he can do what he wanted to do all along. And what he wants to do is show how much he loves us.

To the people of Malachi's day, who thought that God had changed his mind and was being unfaithful in his word, the prophet says, God has not changed. You are loved. That is the word of the Lord to every believer, even the backslider, God loves you. You may have wandered from him, you may have become discouraged and cast your eyes towards the world, but he has not changed. Malachi says, *'You, O descendants of Jacob, are not destroyed'* (3:6) In other words, you would have been destroyed, but because you are loved you are not destroyed. It is only by the Lord's mercies that we are not consumed.

Malachi refers to the people as descendants of Jacob for two reasons apart from the plain fact that they are children of Israel. One, they were being too much like Jacob. He was the heel, the supplanter; he was not a very nice guy. He was the kind of man we love to hate. Two, Jacob had a time of backsliding in his life. And at that time God said, *'I am God Almighty; be fruitful and increase in number. A nation and a community of nations will come from you, and kings will come from your body. The land I gave to Abraham and Isaac I also give to you, and I will give this land to your descendants after you'* (Gen. 35:11-12). What God did there was focus Jacob on himself.

Throughout my ministry I wanted to be utterly allergic to man-centred preaching. I wanted my preaching to be God-centred. This passage from Malachi could not be more God-centred because it focuses entirely on him. The prophet reminds the people that God is not like a man who lies and who changes. Perhaps you are the victim of somebody you thought was a friend and who changed his mind about the friendship. Or perhaps someone you were close to and trusted has changed and become cold and distant. People who had a mother or father who was not faithful in love cannot imagine a God who is. But God is not fickle; he does not have mood swings. The same God who called you to himself when you heard the message that Jesus died on the cross for your sins has not changed; he still loves you. But perhaps you have changed; perhaps something has happened to you. You may have gone off the rails, tiptoeing into the world and beginning to live the kind of life you lived before you were saved, and now you think God cannot possibly love you. But he does; he loves you because he does not change.

Another reason why God's word to Jacob is important is that it shows God's love for him is everlasting; and that is true for every single person who becomes a member of the family of God. You are a child of Jacob by the Holy Spirit, part of a family that goes back for thousands of years. And to be part of this family means to have security for all eternity. Once we are saved we are always saved. We are adopted into the family; we are children of God and joint heirs with Christ. How secure do you suppose Jesus is in the Trinity? How secure is Jesus in the Godhead? Is there any possibility that God the Father would reject his Son and put him out of the Trinity? That is how secure we are. We are loved with an everlasting love. *"Return faithless people," declares the* LORD, *"For I am your husband"'* (Jer. 3:14). The Authorised Version says, *'I am married to the backslider.'* Malachi 3:6-7 shows the consistency of God's love. But although God does not stop loving us, and our eternal destiny is secure, the backslider forfeits the promise of immediate blessing.

In what ways is God unchanging? Firstly, he is unchanging in his promise. *'Praise be to the* LORD, *who has given rest to his people Israel just as he promised. Not one word has failed of all the good promises he gave through his servant Moses'* (I Kings 8:56). Perhaps you feel so guilty and you think you can never forgive yourself for backsliding. God knows how you feel, and he has such a brilliant way of making everything that has happened work together for good that one day you may be tempted to say that it was supposed to be that way. But the fact that God works everything together for good doesn't mean that what you did was right at the time, rather it shows that the Lord restores the years which the locusts have eaten.

Secondly, God is unchanging in regard to his presence. In Matthew's gospel the last words of Jesus are, *'Surely I am with you always, to the very end of the age'* (28:20). *'Your word, O LORD, is eternal; it stands firm in the heavens. Your faithfulness continues through all generations ...'* (Ps. 119:89-90). *'God has said, "Never will I leave you; never will I forsake you"'* (Heb. 13:5). While Jim Bakker, the television preacher, was in prison, he made a study of that verse from Hebrews, in its original Greek. He had not been brought up to believe that Christians are once saved, always saved, but he discovered it from that verse while he was in prison. The Greek literally reads, if you were to draw out its conclusion, 'I will never, never, never, never, never, leave you.' Up to that time Jim felt so unloved because he had let God down, although it turned out that he was falsly accused though there were things he had done wrong. In the end of the day he even thanked God for putting him in prison, saying that it was the best thing that could ever have happened to him because God showed him he was always with him and so gave him a second chance and a new future. That is what God promises to backsliders. He promises his presence. There is, however, a distinction between the certainty of his presence and the sense of his presence. The certainty of his presence is that God says he is with you. His presence is a fact whether you are aware of him or not. But backsliders lose the sense of his presence. When you are not where you ought to be you will not feel the sense of his presence. Sometimes God lets life get pretty dark and miserable in order to make us call on him.

Thirdly, God is unchanging with regard to his purpose. Job felt deserted. He was rejected by all his theologically sound friends, and he had no evidence at all to show that God loved him. The bottom line of the book of Job is, *'I know that you can do all things; no plan of yours can be thwarted'* (42:2). When God spoke to the backsliding Jacob, he told him to go back to Bethel. Why did he do that? Things had gone completely wrong in Jacob's life. His family was in disarray, he was out of sorts, and no-one could reach him. He was unreachable, untouchable and unteachable when God got through to him and told him to go back to Bethel where he had first met with the Lord and found him true.

God still says the same to backsliders, not in terms of returning to the physical place where they were converted, because that could be the other side of the world, but symbolically. Jacob literally went back to Bethel and God met with him again. As a result the man got rid of his foreign gods and purified himself. For backsliders going back to Bethel simply means renewing their vows, finding God as real as they first found him.

Abraham features in one third of Hebrews 11, the great chapter on faith. Moses gets quite a bit, and Jacob, whose name is mentioned more than any of them in the Old Testament, gets one verse. But he is there. *'By faith Jacob, when he was dying ... worshipped as he leaned on the top of his staff'* (Heb. 11:21). Jacob was afraid that he had grieved the Lord over the years, that he had been the world's worst father, the world's greatest manipulator. Over and over again he was full of unbelief and he let God down so much. Then God saved his family without Jacob raising a finger. You can picture him at the end of his life leaning on his staff and saying, 'Every word you promised came true, every word,' and worshipping. God is determined to get all the glory and he does things in our lives so that we cannot take his glory away. *'I am the Lord, that is my name, my glory will I not give to another.'*

Fourthly, God is unchanging in his provision. What ensures our salvation? It is God who keeps us through the blood of Jesus. If you can begin to conceive what the blood of Jesus does for God the Father you will never once doubt that those who are once saved are always saved. Don't think your works can save you, they cannot. And God doesn't like it when you trust your works, your baptism or your church membership. He doesn't like it when you say, 'I have tried to live a good life.' Our only hope, our one and only hope, is the blood of Jesus.

17

Coming Home

"Ever since the time of your forefathers you have turned away from my decrees and have not kept them. Return to me, and I will return to you,' says the LORD Almighty. But you ask, 'How are we to return?' (Malachi 3:7)

According to Malachi the reason these people were not destroyed was because God doesn't change. As the Authorised Version of the Bible says, *'The reason you are not consumed is because I don't change.'* They had been so wayward, and had wandered so far away from what they were taught, that if God were not an unchanging God he would have destroyed them long ago. Circumstances don't alter God's commitment, where men are faithful only as long as somebody is pleasing them. God loves with an everlasting love and his mercy lasts forever. This is something we find in the psalms again and again; it is the most comforting and wonderful word.

The Jews in Malachi's day just repeated history. God says to them, *'Ever since the time of your forefathers you have turned away from my decrees and have not kept them.'* That is what their parents did, and their parents did what their parents did, and it just kept going on. It is the same today. Despite that, each generation always thinks it is better than those that have gone before. Jesus put it like this, *'Woe to you, teachers of the law and Pharisees, you hypocrites! You build tombs for the prophets and decorate the graves of the righteous. And you say,*

"If we had lived in the days of our forefathers, we would not have taken part with them in shedding the blood of the prophets"' (Matt. 23:29-30). Or, as Stephen put it when he was before the Sanhedrin. *'You are just like your fathers: You always resist the Holy Spirit! Was there ever a prophet your fathers did not persecute?'* (Acts 7:51-52). So Malachi comes to them with God's word, *'Return to me, and I will return to you.'*

If you are a backslider, although you are loved you are miserable and you should come back home right now. Coming back home means returning to God's will. Home is the comfort zone; it is where we are secure. I remember years ago hearing Billy Graham on the radio every night at ten o'clock. On Sunday nights after Billy preached, George Beverley Shea sang,

> I've wandered far away from God
> but now I'm coming home;
> the paths of sin too long I've trod,
> Lord, I'm coming home.
> Coming home, coming home,
> never more to roam;
> open wide thine arms of love,
> Lord, I'm coming home.

I would define home as the feeling of being at ease because you are in the centre of God's will. This is the most wonderful feeling in the world as far as I know. As I write this I believe I am in the centre of God's will. He might show me something tomorrow afternoon that needs correcting but, as of this moment, I have walked in every ray of light I know. I have made every correction I can think of and God has dealt with me. But when I think of how merciful God has been to me, and how much he knows about me, and how he has stayed with me, I am so indebted to him that I have no choice but to be obedient.

There are three reasons why this is important to us. Firstly, can you think of reasons God should have let you go a long time ago? Can you think of a reason he should have dropped you and started all over again with somebody else? But he didn't drop you in spite of all you have done, and all that has gone wrong and all that has been swept under the carpet. God still asks you to come home, to return to him and he will return to you.

Secondly, this word shows the folly of not learning from history. That is why he says. *'Ever since the time of your forefathers you have turned away from my decrees and have not kept them'* (3:7). They had not learned from history, in fact they repeated history. The German philosopher, Hagel, concluded that the only thing we seem to have learned from history is that we do not learn from history. People make the same mistakes over and over again. I have watched younger people make the same mistakes I made. We all seem to have to learn for ourselves, to get our own fingers burnt. You may say of your mistakes that you are not the first to make them and that you are in good company. Jesus told the Pharisees, who said that if they had lived in the days of their forefathers they would not have made the mistakes their forefathers made, that they were doing exactly the same things.

God says he is going to come suddenly to his temple, and he asks who can endure the day of his coming, who can stand when he appears? That will be an awful moment. I think hell can be defined partly as eternal loneliness. I feel blessed because I am so glad I am not going to hell. God has saved me because my sins are washed by the blood of Jesus. I am not trusting in my own righteousness; it would be foolish to do that. Instead my trust is in what Jesus did for me on the cross. If you are not saved don't be a fool by saying that you will be in great company in hell. That may be true, but you won't be conscious of it. All will be darkness because it will be as though you are all by yourself. You will cry out for mercy and it will be too late. Don't go to hell. The Bible in a nutshell is found in John 3:16, *'For God so loved the world that he gave his one and only Son, that whoever believes in him shall not perish but have eternal life.'*

Thirdly, the Lord does not change. He has kept you alive to bring you back. God has brought you to this point of your life to waken you up because he loves you, because he is not finished with you. It is, as the New English Bible translates this verse, *'You have not ceased to be the sons of Jacob because I don't change.'* People change, God says, but I don't change. This is the foundation of the teaching that Christians are once saved, always saved. God does not change. Or as another translator puts it, *'I the Lord have not gone back on my word.'*

God's accusation in this verse is that *'you have turned away from my decrees.'* What does the word 'decree' mean? A decree is a judgement or decision. In psalm 119 there are seven words that can be used interchangeably: law, statutes, precepts, decrees, commands, word and promises. All these refer to the revealed will of God. When people come to me asking how they can know God's will, I tell them it is in the Bible. If you were stranded on a remote desert island with only five pages from the Bible there would be enough in those five pages, wherever they came from, to give you a glimpse of what God wants of you and how he wants you to live your life. That psalm concludes with, *'I have strayed like a lost sheep. Seek your servant...'* (Ps. 119:176).

Two final points: How these people wandered and how they could come home. They wandered because they turned away from God's word. How do you turn from God's word? First you stop praying. You can remember days when you took time to pray, but then you became busy, busy, busy. You think that God understands that you were too tired to pray, but eventually not praying doesn't seem to bother you any more. Next you stopped reading the Bible. The devil doesn't want you to read the Bible and he will come up with every reason why you don't need to. He'll make you keep putting off regular Bible reading till you find yourself in a most precarious state.

Then you begin to yield to temptation. Now what is temptation for some may not be temptation for another. For some it may be drink, for another it may be sex, for another it may be pornography. You begin to yield to temptation, and by this time you feel too ashamed to pray and you feel too ashamed to read the Bible. The fourth thing that happens is that you return to a life not dissimilar to what you were converted from. At first that bothers you, but after a while you become anaesthetised to it and you almost feel at home even though you are a long way from home. That is how you wander from God.

How do we make our way back home? Firstly, you have to recognise where home is. It is the centre of God's will; it is those decrees, statutes, precepts, laws, word, promises and statutes. The Bible tells you what God wants and how to live your life. That is how you begin to find your way back home. Secondly, admit how far from home you are. Don't play games with yourself. Admit you have become cold inside, that your attitude is not right. Thirdly, know that God loves you. In the parable of the prodigal son, the young man decides to *'go back to my father and say to him: "Father, I have sinned against heaven and against you. I am no longer worthy to be called your son'* (Luke 15:18). Why would he think of doing that? He thought of doing it because he knew he was loved. And even if you are a backslider you are still loved. God, who made you so that you will only be happy when you are in his will and utterly miserable out of it, is asking you to come home. Fourthly, you have to admit what is wrong. In Malachi's day people had no sense of shame, but the way home is to admit what you are ashamed of, what you have done, and what you have become. It is to come to terms with what you know is true. Sometimes it can be helpful to spill out your heart to another Christian but the main thing is that you sort it out with God. Fifthly, you need to ask for mercy. The son said to his father, *'I have sinned against heaven and against you. I am no longer worthy to be called your son'* (Luke 15:21). When you ask for mercy you know you have no bargaining power. You can't snap your finger and tell God that he has to do this for you.

Years ago, when Louise and I, with TR and Melissa, went back to Ashland, Kentucky, on holiday, I couldn't wait to go to the house in which I lived from the age of four until I was seventeen, the year my mother died. But when I found it, I discovered the owners had changed the house all around. I thought, how dare they do that! It wasn't home. You can't go back to things in this world, but you can come back into the will of God and he will bring you home. As the old song says, 'I've wasted many precious years, but now I'm coming home. I now repent with bitter tears, Lord I'm coming home.'

18

IS IT THE PRINCIPLE
OR IS IT THE MONEY?

'Ever since the time of your forefathers you have turned away from my decrees and have not kept them. Return to me, and I will return to you,' says the LORD Almighty. 'But you ask, "How are we to return?" Will a man rob God? Yet you rob me. But you ask, "How do we rob you?" In tithes and offerings. You are under a curse – the whole nation of you – because you are robbing me. Bring the whole tithe into the storehouse, that there may be food in my house. Test me in this,' says the LORD Almighty, 'and see if I will not throw open the floodgates of heaven and pour out so much blessing that you will not have room enough for it. I will prevent pests from devouring your crops, and the vines in your fields will not cast their fruit,' says the LORD Almighty' (Malachi 3:7-11).

The first question is, 'How have you loved us?' Malachi gives the answer. Second question, 'How have we despised your name?' Malachi gives the answer. Third question, 'Why doesn't God accept our offering?' Malachi answers. Next question, 'How have we made God tired?' Malachi answers. Then the question, 'How are we to return?' Malachi says, 'Since you asked I'll tell you.' He tells them that it has something to do with money.

The French atheist Voltaire, once said cynically, 'When it comes to a man's wallet every person's religion is the same.' He said that Christians are no different from non-Christians when it comes to money, and I have to say he has a point. I know many people who call themselves Christians who get very nervous when you talk about money. John Wesley said that the last part of a person to be converted is his wallet or pocket book. We get so indignant about money that we want to turn it into a principle. I have had people say to me that it is not the money it is the principle. Well I am going to give you eleven principles on the subject of tithing.

Principle one, money is the gift of God. It is part of what theologians call 'common grace', not common in the sense that it is ordinary, but in the sense that it is given commonly to everybody, even those not saved, even those who will never be saved. If it weren't for God's common grace the world would become topsy-turvy; there would be utter chaos. The very fact that there is order in the universe, the fact that there is such a thing as a violin concerto, proves the existence of common grace.

Principle two, your job is a gift from God. How often do you thank God for your job? How often do you thank him that you have income? You should do so because God gave you your job. I know of people who just took their jobs for granted until suddenly they lost them. Then they realised they had thought the world owed them a living. But God himself had given them a source of income. Thank God for your job.

Principle three, the ability to earn money is a gift. In some ways it is an exceedingly rare gift. I am not saying the ability to spend money is a gift, you do not need to do any kind of course on how to spend money. We all love to spend it if we have it. You see something you need, or think you need, and you just can't resist buying it. The worst thing that can happen to some people is that they are given a credit card. They behave as though things cost nothing. He that is faithful in that which is least is faithful also in much. Learn to handle money.

Principle four, God puts us on our honour to show gratitude. Now gratitude, saying thank you, pleases God. We all like it if we do something for a person and he comes and says, 'Thank you', we say, 'Don't mention it,' but we are glad he did. And when God does something for us he wants us to thank him. When Jesus healed ten lepers and only one said thank you, Jesus asked where the other nine were because he knew all ten had been healed. God notices when we say thank you. Now for a very important theological point - you are not in a position to say thank you to God until you have been saved. The reformed doctrine of sanctification has been called the doctrine of gratitude. Living a holy life is living a life that says thank you to God, and only those who are saved can do that.

Principle five, one way, not the only way, but one way we say thank you to God is by giving. Giving does not earn your salvation. You could give a million pounds and still not be saved.

Principle six, pleasing God, showing thanks, is not limited to what you and I may want to call spiritual things: worship, prayer, sound theology, being busy in the church, witnessing on the streets, or morality and faithfulness in marriage. Pleasing God is not limited to those things. There is more to pleasing God than faithfulness in attendance, faithfulness in marriage, faithfulness in Bible reading and faithfulness in witnessing. There are some people who assume that is all there is to it and, when it comes to the area of money, there is a little sign saying that no trespassing is allowed. It is a no-go area and they don't like anybody intruding into it. Imagine your hands folded and somebody coming and tying a rubber band in different directions all over your hands. You try to open your hands and you just can't. You struggle to be free but you can't release your hands until someone cuts the rubber band and releases them. There are people like that when it comes to money; they are in bondage. But they don't realise their need to be set free. It is amazing what happens when a person like that begins to give.

Principle seven, there is an inseparable connection between your money and your relationship with God. *Whoever keeps the whole law and yet stumbles at just one point is guilty of breaking all of it'* (Jam. 2:10). We think of different commandments: you shall have no other gods before me, you shall not commit adultery, you shall not steal, you shall not bear false witness, honour your father and mother, and so on, and you could say you had kept them all. But then there is the tithe. What is that? That is one tenth of your income. A tenth of all God gives you is his alone. You cannot enjoy the fullness of God's blessing and avoid the issue of money. Until your money is under the blood of Jesus, which means that you recognise what he allows you to keep for yourself and what he regards as his own, and you give his back to him, your relationship with God will not be right.

Principle eight, Christians who do not give what God tells them to give sooner or later suffer both financially and spiritually. I have known Christians who were in debt and who were not tithing, their view being that when they got out of debt they would tithe. They would argue that it was a poor Christian testimony to give money to the church but not pay their bills. I understand why they say that because I was in that position many years ago before Louise and I were married. I was in debt and I reckoned I should pay my bills first because that is what is honouring to God. Two years later I was even deeper in debt. Then I started tithing, I was still in debt but I started tithing. I didn't get out of debt in one week, but I did in two years and I learned my lesson.

Principle nine, God has told us how much to give. Don't go up to someone who has a gift of prophecy and say, 'Do you have a word for me? How do you feel the Lord wants me to give?' If you are waiting for some word of knowledge to tell you how much you ought to give, here it is - you should tithe. The tithe is the Lord's own possession. *'A tithe of everything from the land, whether grain from the soil or fruit from the trees, belongs to the LORD; it is holy to the LORD'* (Lev. 27:30). You might tell me that tithing is of the law and we are not under the law. I answer that Abraham was the first tither, and the law hadn't even been given when he was alive. The law legalised what Abraham did voluntarily. We are not under the law but we do go back to Abraham. While tithing doesn't get you into heaven, it is a way of saying thank you to God.

Principle ten, one source of backsliding is robbing God. Malachi asks, *'Will a man rob God?'* When God gives you ten pounds, one pound is his. If you give him fifty pence you have robbed him of the other fifty pence. If he gives you ten thousand pounds and you give him five hundred pounds you have robbed him of five hundred pounds. The tithe belongs to the Lord and God puts us on our honour to give it to him. Since the tithe belongs to the Lord what you keep of that is robbing him. The Inland Revenue doesn't put you on your honour, they have ways of getting your money. God just puts you on your honour.

Principle eleven, returning to God partly consists of stopping robbing him of what is his due. It is not the only thing, you cannot continue to live in adultery and think tithing will make you right with God, nor can you continue to hold a grudge and tithe to sort it out. But returning to God requires tithing. It is not the money, it is the principle. And I've given you eleven principles to start you off on the subject of tithing.

19

CAN WE PROVE GOD?

'Bring the whole tithe into the storehouse, that there may be food in my house. Test me in this,' says the LORD Almighty, 'and see if I will not throw open the floodgates of heaven and pour out so much blessing that you will not have room enough for it' (Malachi 3:10).

The Bible never attempts to prove God. It is God's book; it is his word. Everything he wanted in it is there, and nothing he didn't want in it is included. God wants people to believe in him but he doesn't try to prove himself. He doesn't start his book with, 'Since this is a book about me, here are the reasons you should believe me and here are the reasons you should know that I am there. In other words, here are the proofs of my existence.' God doesn't do that. The Bible just begins with the words, *'In the beginning God'* (Gen. 1:1). That is it.

In the Middle Ages scholastic theologians worked out proofs of God and they were very popular even though they only proved the existence of God to those who were already convinced that he is. But there is no proof of God that will cause an unbeliever suddenly to believe that he exists. Similarly, there is no proof that the Bible is the word of God though there are what we call external proofs of the Bible. Some go into archaeology to verify biblical facts, and there are archaeological evidences for the validity of the Bible. Others use the fact that the Bible has changed so many lives to show that it is God's word. Charles Spurgeon used to say, 'Defend the Bible? I would as soon defend a lion.' For reasons we do not understand, God has chosen not to prove himself and not to prove that the Bible his word.

The closest he comes to proving himself is in these verses from Malachi when God says, *'Test me in this ... and see if I will not throw open the floodgates of heaven.'* God tells the people that if they want to prove that he exists they should bring the whole tithe into the storehouse and watch what he does. He puts his integrity on the line. God doesn't give philosophical proofs, rather he gives a way in which we can prove him. Elsewhere in the Bible we are told not to put God to the test (Deut. 6:16, Matt. 4:7) but these verses carry a different meaning. They teach us not to test God, e.g. not to do something stupid like jumping off a tower assuming that God will keep us from harm. This testing of God is very different. This verse was given to motivate backslidden Israelites to return to God, and it was to be done through tithing. Today God continues to challenge us regarding our money.

This verse teaches us six things. One, the Israelites of Malachi's day were backslidden because they were withholding from God what was his. I would do you no favour to withhold this teaching from you. I have had people come to me a year or two after hearing me preach on tithing to thank me for what I said. The reason that most Christians don't tithe is that they have not been taught to; they don't know what God expects of them.

Two, the entire nation was under a curse because God's people were robbing him. Malachi says that a dark gloomy cloud is hanging over Israel and it is traceable to the fact that God is angry at being robbed. By how much is God being robbed in our land today? Can you imagine what would happen if every believer tithed? Churches that are emptying would suddenly fill and, more than that, I believe it would affect the whole nation spiritually. The gloom that darkens our country would lift. The difference would be profound. We have a responsibility to God that, if we fulfilled it, would change our nation.

Three, God wants all that is due to him. It is not enough for you to give him a part, even a large part. That is not what he says. God says he wants it all and he wants it week by week. It doesn't mean you can tithe every second month and save for a rainy day the months in between. How would you like it if your husband or wife said, 'I am going to be faithful this month but next month I think maybe I will have an affair'? That is how many Christians think when it comes to God's money. They wouldn't dream of committing adultery but, when it comes to money, they split God's tithe between him and other things. And we wonder why we are under a cloud!

Four, the tithe should go to the storehouse. Now everybody knew then what that was, it was the synagogue or the temple. Today it means the church, your church. In Malachi's day the synagogue was local, today the storehouse is your local church. That is God's plan. Nowadays we have countless para-church organizations and they need to be supported by Christians. But these should be supported either by local churches or by Christians who have already given a tenth of their income to their own church. Their support of para-church organisations should be over and above their tithe. If everybody gave to the storehouse, missionaries could be supported with ease and there would be no limit to what we could give to other worthy causes.

Five, the purpose of storehouse tithing is that there would be food or meat in God's house. What does he mean by food? It could mean literal food. If the Levites who lived off the tithes of the people had food then God would bless the whole nation. Today it is in reverse. Clergy are among the lowest paid professions where in the days of the Levites they were given the best. Or it may be referring to spiritual food. The worst thing that can happen, says the prophet Amos, is for there to be a famine in the land, and by famine he meant a famine of God's word. If every minister were supported in the way God wants him to be supported it would result in teaching that would edify.

Today there is so little teaching because people are not tithing and they have no appetite for deep teaching. But when a person begins to give to God, something is unlocked within him and he has a love for the Lord. The Spirit begins to flood his soul and he can't get enough teaching.

Six, God challenges us to discover for ourselves why this is true, and that it is true. Think of this: God is angry with those who rob him yet he tenderly stoops to where we are to motivate us to give. That is why he tells us to test him. God challenges us here. But he doesn't challenge us to tithe for a trial period to see what happens. I once got a letter from a lady saying that she had started tithing the previous week and a bill came from the Inland Revenue for £700. She concluded that she wasn't supposed to tithe! Tithing is not like that. It is a commitment, a life sentence. I was brought up in a working class family. Dad made eight dollars a day, forty dollars a week. He gave four dollars to the church and we lived on thirty-six. He told us that the thirty-six dollars would go as far as the forty, maybe further. The man who underwrote our Oxford tuition told me that, when he was young and in debt, he came across the words, 'Those who honour me I will honour' (I Sam. 2:30). He made a covenant with God to tithe from that day and he never looked back. I am only one of those he has been able to bless with financial support.

While tithing is of huge importance, no-one will be saved just by tithing. Tithing is not how you become a Christian. You are saved when you realise that God sent his Son into the world to die on a cross, to shed his blood, to do for you what you can't do – keep the law perfectly. By the way, the fact that Jesus kept the law means that he tithed. When you trust Jesus, his righteousness is put to your credit. It follows that in God's sight you are a tither because you are covered by his righteousness. You will go to heaven even though you have never tithed, and you will stay saved even if you don't become a tither because tithing is not what guarantees salvation. The connection between spirituality and money is that when you don't give God what is his, you don't grow spiritually and you may also suffer financially. Your Christian life just won't be the same.

20

Unlocking the Gates of Heaven

'Bring the whole tithe into the storehouse, that there may be food in my house. Test me in this,' says the Lord Almighty, 'and see if I will not throw open the floodgates of heaven and pour out so much blessing that you will not have room enough for it. I will prevent pests from devouring your crops, and the vines in your fields will not cast their fruit,' said the Lord Almighty. 'Then all the nations will call you blessed, for yours will be a delightful land,' says the Lord Almighty (Malachi 3:10-12).

We come now to the phrase, *'unlocking the gates of heaven.'* I wonder if you secretly wish that somehow you could unlock the gates of heaven. God has been hiding his face from you, or things have not been going well for you, and you just want something to come directly from God to you. Malachi tells us how this can happen. A few weeks after Louise and I were married I was deep in debt and I wasn't tithing. I was depressed working as a salesman and not bringing in much, certainly not enough to clear my debts. I prayed, 'Lord I don't feel your presence. I can't go on. Please speak to me.' Louise kept putting on the table a white big Bible that my grandmother McCurley had given us for our wedding gift. It was open, and as I went to read it I prayed, 'Lord please let it be open at a place that will give me some comfort.' As I looked down my eyes fell on these words, *'Will a man rob God? Yet you rob me. But you ask, "How do we rob you?" In tithes and offerings'* (Mal. 3:8). I felt so angry that I just closed that Bible and turned on the television we still owed money on. 'Lord I wanted you to give me a blessing,' I complained. But I couldn't shake off those words. And I am glad about that because I learned some lessons that are still with me.

One, not tithing did not forfeit my salvation. Christians are once saved, always saved. And if there is any truth we should cling to, it is that one.

Two, God did not cease to love me because I failed to tithe. We are loved with an everlasting love; God's love for his people just doesn't stop. Even the best of people like us as long as we please them; they like us as long as we do things for them. We are not able to grasp God's kind of love. Even though I was robbing him God kept on loving me. The theme of the book of Malachi is *You are loved*. God didn't stop loving the Israelites even though they were stealing for him. Why else would he give them this word? Why else would he bother to speak to them about their robbery? And God's message is the same today. How do you respond to it? Some react to this subject by digging in their heels, saying that they don't think they agree. When God spoke to me about it I was so angry I closed the Bible. I didn't want that kind of word; I wanted encouragement. But that was God's word for me and it was what I needed. I didn't walk in the light that first day but eventually I did, and I pray that my testimony will plant a seed in your mind.

Three, robbing God did not stop his gracious guidance in my life. He still led me. You may not be a tither and yet you still sense that God is with you and blessing you in many, many ways. It is because God is so gracious that many decide not to tithe, because he still loves them, he still guides them, he still takes care of them and he still gives them the assurance of eternal salvation.

What did robbing God do in my experience? First, he withheld financial blessing. Even though I reasoned that I shouldn't tithe while I was repaying my debts, two years later I was even deeper in debt than before. God doesn't always get at us through financial reverse, but he may well do that to get our attention.

Second, God withheld spiritual insight and intimacy. A year or so before God spoke to me, I had such intimacy with him. The Holy Spirit was so real that the sense of his presence and his peace and joy were indescribable. But somehow things went wrong and I grieved the Holy Spirit by becoming too interested in material things. Before I knew it I was deep in debt. Kendall was such a good name in the area that I was able to run up all sorts of bills.

Third, God locked the windows of heaven. It is he who controls the floodgates of heaven. In Malachi's day that meant that God controlled the weather, because the floodgates of heaven then meant rain. Israel needs rain, and it gets it so rarely that when it rains the people thank God for the rain. God could get their attention by stopping the floodgates of heaven, by not sending rain. But it also means that the Lord controls material and spiritual blessing, including the blessing of the Holy Spirit. This passage teaches us that if we want things to change we must get on good terms with God. It won't do to plant seed if there is no rain. So if you know God and bypass what he says in his word, you are being foolish and you cannot expect his showers of blessing.

When you have felt a lack of his blessing you might have thought that the way to unlock the gates of heaven was to double up on your prayer life. That could do you no harm, but that is not what he says here. You might think that what you need is to have an all-night prayer meeting. God doesn't say that. Maybe you thought you should start fasting twice a week to get the sense of his presence. But God doesn't say that either. What he says is, 'Bring the whole tithe.' And if you do that the blessing promised is immense. God says that he will open the floodgates of heaven and pour out so many blessings that you will not have room enough for them.

This text also teaches that as the church goes, so goes the nation. *Then all the nations will call you blessed, for yours will be a delightful land* (3:12). In Malachi's day there was a curse over the nation that was traceable to the church. The people of God were impoverished and that was traceable to the ministry. And the impoverished ministry was traceable to people robbing God. Elsewhere God says, *Whoever sows sparingly will also reap sparingly, and whoever sows generously will also reap generously* (2 Cor. 9:6). How much could be unlocked in your life if you were to remember that and work on it? A few verses further on God says, *You will be made rich in every way so that you can be generous on every occasion, and through us your generosity will result in thanksgiving to God* (2 Cor. 9:11). John Bunyan, who wrote *Pilgrim's Progress*, also wrote this. 'There was a man, some called him mad, the more he gave the more he had.'

What we have in this passage is motivation by encouragement followed by motivation by warning. The encouragement is that you are going to be blessed. It amazes me that God bothers to encourage when he could have just hammered the people with the law. He stoops to their weakness, telling them that although they have been robbing him if they start giving him what is his own he will wonderfully bless them. *No eye has seen, no ear has heard, no mind has conceived what God has prepared for those who love him* (1 Cor. 2:9). But there is also a warning. God has a way of collecting the tithe in order to rebuke us. In other words, either we tithe voluntarily or God takes it in other ways.

There is a story of a church with one hundred and fifty members. Another pastor asked the pastor of the church how many of his members tithed. He said, 'One hundred and fifty.' 'One hundred and fifty members and one hundred and fifty tithers?' the other man said, astonished. 'Yes,' the pastor explained. 'About fifty of them give a tithe to God voluntarily and he takes it from the rest.'

Those who do not tithe voluntarily could actually be under a curse. *'You are under a curse' (3:9)*, God said to the whole nation. Imagine our nation being under a cloud that was traceable to the church, traceable to our robbing God. If every Christian would take this seriously the church would be transformed and so would the nation.

21

DOES GOD HAVE FEELINGS?

"You have said harsh things against me,' says the LORD. 'Yet you ask, '"What have we said against you?" You have said, "It is futile to serve God. What did we gain by carrying out his requirements and going about like mourners before the LORD Almighty? But now we call the arrogant blessed. Certainly the evildoers prosper, and even those who challenge God escape"' (Malachi 3:13-15).

Malachi changes the subject from that of tithing to the issue of God's justice. He has just said that the nation was under a curse because his people were not tithing; they were not bringing God's due to his storehouse and so were not receiving his blessing. But they challenged what he said. They did not believe it. They said that serving God did not do them any good. Interestingly, when Malachi changes the subject to that of God's justice, he is actually returning to a subject he has already addressed in 2:17. *'You have wearied the LORD with your words. "How have we wearied him?" you ask. By saying, "All who do evil are good in the eyes of the LORD, and he is pleased with them" or "Where is the God of justice?"'* This has been such a bone of contention, such a sore spot, that Malachi actually comes back to the subject.

Why does Malachi come back to this subject after speaking about tithing? The answer is that probably the single most common complaint that God ever hears is, Why does God allow evil? Why does God allow suffering? The most common reason people give for doubting the existence of God is the fact of human suffering. They say, 'If God exists why does he allow suffering? Why did God create the world in which evil is a possibility?' A theologian asked me many years ago, 'Why did God create man knowing he would suffer?' This is why David says as he sees wicked men prosper, *Do not fret because of evil men or be envious of those who do wrong'* (Ps. 37:1). And Habakkuk asks, *'Why do you make me look at injustice? Why do you tolerate wrong?'* (Hab. 1:3). By creating a world in which evil was not only a possibility, but one in which man would inevitably suffer, God himself opened the way for the most harsh and hard questions imaginable even though he knew in advance what people would say.

Over all my years of ministry I have only found two answers to these harsh questions. The first is that we do not know the answer and anybody who says he does is a fool. God has made it impossible for us to know, so if we are going to spend our time trying to figure out why he allows evil we are wasting our time. He has designed the whole matter in such a manner that you cannot know why.

But there is a second answer, and as far as I know it is the nearest you get to the answer you want, and I am sure it is a correct one. That is that God allows these things in order to make faith a possibility. Faith, to be faith, is believing God without the evidence; faith, to be faith, is relying on God without having all our questions answered. If we knew all the answers we would not need to have faith. But God chose to save a people for himself that would accept his word, trust his integrity and believe the Bible that he has given us. If you give any thought to the crucifixion you will realise how fully God understands the problems of suffering and apparent injustice, because there was nothing fair about what happened to Jesus. Think of the details of the so-called trial of Jesus. But that is not all, God's decree that his Son should die on a cross appears to be the most foolish and ridiculous nonsense, yet it is the greatest thing that has ever happened. Let the cross be a hint about how God will one day clear his name.

The question here is, when God hears the kind of criticism Malachi calls 'harsh words' does he care? The answer is that he does. The proof is in these verses. If he didn't care he wouldn't have told them. This tells us two things. One, God hears our conversations. Two, God has feelings. Why are these facts important?

Firstly, because of what some call the impassability of God, which means that God doesn't ever feel any kind of suffering. Suffering doesn't affect him. The English have a stiff upper lip but that doesn't mean they don't feel, they just don't show their feelings. There are some who believe in the impassibility of God as strongly as they believe in his power, his wisdom and his omnipresence. I don't believe it. I believe that God does have feelings. Because he loves our praise it follows that he doesn't like being criticised.

Secondly, God takes notice of what we say about him and he feels it. The very fact that God told them that he heard their harsh words shows he cares, that he loves them too much not to tell them. He takes notice of what we say. Have you said harsh things about the Lord? The Bible says, *'If we confess our sins, he is faithful and just and will forgive us our sins and purify us from all unrighteousness'* (I John 1:9).

Thirdly, the knowledge that God hears, that he cares and that he has feelings, should change how we live and speak. We should watch our words. *'I said, "I will watch my ways and keep my tongue from sin; I will put a muzzle on my mouth as long as the wicked are in my presence"'* (Ps. 39:1). God hears; God is listening; let us watch what we say about him and about other people too. Jesus said, *'You brood of vipers, how can you who are evil say anything good? For out of the overflow of the heart the mouth speaks ... But I tell you that men will have to give account on the day of judgment for every careless word they have spoken'* (Matt. 12: 34, 36). Confess your evil words and your careless words now and they will not be held against you then.

Some other points about this verse. One, if God did not care about us he would not bother to warn us when we go wrong. The proof we are on speaking terms with him is that he warns us. There was no warning to Sodom and Gomorrah; God just wiped them off the earth.

Two, God takes it personally when we ask why we should obey him? R. T. Williams, the man I was named after, tells the story of a businessman who made $1m dollars. He tithed it and had receipts for $100,000 that he had given to the church. Later, when he went bankrupt, someone asked if he wouldn't like to have that $100,000 back? 'Oh, no, oh no,' he said, 'that is the only amount I kept; the Lord got that.' Have you ever asked what you gained by carrying out his requirements? Have you ever thought it was futile to serve God when you look around and see even blasphemers seeming to be blessed? If you have said these things God will not hold it against you if you come back to him and tell him you are truly sorry.

Three, it is one thing for unrighteousness people and wicked people to talk like these Israelites, but for those who are in the family it should be out of the question. For a Christian to lapse into this way of thinking, and to start giving voice to the most fundamental complaint of the non-Christian, should be out of the question. We are not called to think the way the natural man thinks because the Christian lives by faith. What is faith? *'Faith is being sure of what we hope for and certain of what we do not see'* (Heb. 11:1).

Four, one day God will clear his name, and when he does that we will all say, 'Why didn't we think of that?' Have you ever read a book that was so cleverly written that you couldn't figure it out until the end? God is doing that. But one day he will clear his name, and those who are going to be happy about it are those who have accepted the problem of suffering by faith rather than because they have all the answers. God will have the last word on the subject. For believers that will be such a happy day.

In the meantime what do we do? Habakkuk ended his prophecy. *'Though the fig-tree does not bud and there are no grapes on the vines, though the olive crops fail and the fields produce no food, though there are no sheep in the pen and no cattle in the stalls, yet I will rejoice in the LORD, I will be joyful in God my Saviour. The Sovereign LORD is my strength; he makes my feet like the feet of a deer, he enables me to go on the heights'* (Hab. 3:17-19). Habakkuk's problems did not go away, but he accepted them by faith and rejoiced. One night, when Arthur Blessit was carrying the cross in Northern Israel, he was cold and had no place to sleep. As he lay on a bench by a bus stop with the cold rain pouring down on him, he said, 'Lord, I rebuke the wind and I rebuke the storm in Jesus' name. Stop it, in the name of Jesus.' When the lightning crashed and the rain still poured on him, Arthur said, 'Lord, I love you anyway.'

22

THE EAVESDROPPING GOD

Then those who feared the LORD talked with each other, and the LORD listened and heard. A scroll of remembrance was written in his presence concerning those who feared the LORD and honoured his name. 'They will be mine,' says the LORD Almighty, 'in the day when I make up my treasured possession. I will spare them, just as in compassion a man spares his son who serves him. And you will again see the distinction between the righteous and the wicked, between those who serve God and those who do not' (Malachi 3:16-18).

I read the Bible over and over again without really seeing what was in verse sixteen until a preacher said, 'The Lord will eavesdrop what you say,' because the Bible says, *'Those who feared the LORD talked with each other and the LORD listened and heard.'* When you that fear the Lord talk with one another and begin to express what you wish the Lord would do, the Lord eavesdrops your conversation and says, I am going to turn that into a prayer; I am going to take that on board and I am going to give that person what he wants.

What does this interesting little verse teach us? One, it shows that there were some Jews in Malachi's day who feared God. We have seen the negative side: they offered unacceptable sacrifices; they were divorcing their wives and marrying foreign women; they weren't tithing and they were complaining that it didn't pay to serve the Lord, that he took so little notice they could be disobedient and still blessed. Now we find out that not everybody was like that; there were those that feared the Lord. Even in churches like the one at Sardis (Rev. 3:1-6) there were those who had not soiled their garments. You can look at church history and see that at low-water marks, when the tide was out, even then God always had a remnant. Today, with church attendance going right down, God still has his people. Even today it is not all dark.

Two, those who feared the Lord found each other and shared together. People who fear the Lord have a way of finding one another, and what they share is what we call fellowship. There is fellowship with God, of course, but there is also the communion that comes when you know someone else believes what you believe, feels what you feel.

Three, the Lord listened; he eavesdropped. How does that make you feel? You may say that this is unfair, that it is like being spied on. When I visited the old Soviet Union with two others in 1974, we had to search our car and our hotel rooms for hidden microphones. Is that like what God is doing? Yes, in a way it is. But he bought us with a price and he has a right to do it. We don't have a right to ourselves; we belong to the Lord.

Four, those who feared the Lord talked with each other and the Lord listened, *and heard.* You might think that is a redundant phrase; if he listened you don't need to add that he heard. If he listened he surely heard, so why bother to say he listened and heard. To understand this you need to know how the Jewish mind worked. There is a Hebrew word *shamar.* Every Jew knows the shamar, 'Hear O Israel the Lord our God is one Lord.' But the word not only means 'to hear', it also means 'to obey'. Only the context shows which meaning. The idea is this: parents sometimes ask their child, 'Did you hear me?' the implication being that they had not heard because they had not obeyed. In Hebrew to hear is also to obey. So if we hear the Lord we obey him, and if the Lord hears us he will obey our requests that conform with his will. Malachi says, *'Those who feared the LORD talked with each other, and the LORD listened and heard.'* This is wonderful! When people who fear the Lord tell each other what they would like to happen, what they would like God to do, he is touched, he is moved; he sees those desires and he feels the pain. And what God did then was to turn those conversations into prayers. I could have called this study, When our conversations become prayers to God.

Why is this important? Firstly, when we know that God eavesdrops it will affect what we say. Sometimes, when you are talking with a friend, someone else comes and you stop talking out of courtesy or change the subject. Keeping that in mind, when you are talking with somebody and you suddenly are aware that God is eavesdropping, would you keep on talking, would you keep saying the same thing? Would you change the subject if you became aware that the Lord was eavesdropping? That is exactly what he is doing, and he is doing it day and night.

Secondly, we should choose to spend our time with people who fear the Lord. Who do you want to be with? On what basis do you make friendships? If you seek someone who fears God when looking for a friend, a partner, or when seeking advice, you will save yourself a lot of trouble. A person is known by the company that he or she keeps.

Thirdly, we may be praying without knowing it. Wouldn't it be something if, when you get to heaven, you find out that the prayer that was answered was one you didn't even know you had prayed. It was a desire you expressed when you were with somebody who feared the Lord. You may not realise it, but by talking to another person who fears the Lord, and sharing your deepest thoughts and needs, God's heart is touched and he hears the conversation as prayer. He listens and hears.

Fourthly, we should be thankful that God eavesdrops on our conversations. You may sometimes think that you would like a little space without God looking at you, listening to you and knowing your thoughts. But it is never like that. The Psalmist said, *'O LORD, you have searched me and you know me. You* know when I sit and when I rise; you perceive my thoughts from afar' (Ps. 139:1-2). Like it or not that is how it is. But knowing that the Lord sees my thoughts means I can have shorthand conversations with him. Even when I can't make myself clear in words, God knows what is in my heart. And it could be in a moment when you are desperate, in a moment when you had not been thinking about God, all of a sudden you need him and you cry out, knowing he is there and listening. And having that awareness in our minds can keep us out of a lot of mischief.

The book of Ecclesiastes ends with these words: 'Now all has been heard; here is the conclusion of the matter: Fear God and keep his commandments, for this is the whole duty of man. For God will bring every deed into judgement, including every hidden thing, whether it is good or evil' (Ecc. 12:13-14). Fear of the Lord makes us respect his ways.

This verse also lets us know something about the Lord's faculties, his mental state. The Lord has faculties, he thinks and he feels. It hurts him to hear harsh things about himself and it make him happy when we choose friends who also fear the Lord and share fellowship with them.

God even hears our faintest whisper. He hangs on our every word. Because he cares so much for us his mind doesn't wander. God, the eavesdropper, is so faithful that he turns our conversations into petitions. When he hears the desire of our hearts, he turns it into a prayer and answers it. That is how God is, and I just love him for it.

23

GOD'S BOOK OF REMEMBRANCE

Then those who feared the LORD talked with each other, and the LORD listened and heard. A scroll of remembrance was written in his presence concerning those who feared the LORD and honoured his name (Malachi 3:16).

In the second part of this verse Malachi uses the interesting expression *'a scroll of remembrance'*. He does not say that God wrote the scroll, I think an angel did it and that it was written in God's presence. I am speculating, but I suspect that is the way it is. Angels are his agents and they write down everything. What is this scroll of remembrance? Moses prayed, *'Please forgive their sin – but if not, then blot me out of the book you have written'* (Ex. 32:32). David prayed, *'May they be blotted out of the book of life and not be listed with the righteous'* (Ps. 69:28). *'The LORD will write in the register of the peoples: "This one was born in Zion"'* (Ps. 87:6). *'At that time your people – everyone whose name is found written in the book – will be delivered'* (Dan. 12:1).

It seems that there was a growing understanding in ancient Israel that God has a book in which the names of the people who fear him are recorded. And the things they talked about are written down too. Jesus said, *'I tell you that men will have to give account on the day of judgment for every careless word they have spoken'* (Matt. 12:36). So two things are recorded: people's names and their conversations. This was an implicit part of Paul's theology. *'Not that I am looking for a gift, but I am looking for what may be credited to your account'* (Phil. 4:17). And those things that are credited to your account add to your reward in heaven.

While every Christian will go to heaven, not all will receive an equal reward there. At the judgment seat of Christ two judgements will be made. The first is the separation of those who will go to heaven and those who will go to hell – *'some to everlasting life, others to shame and everlasting contempt'* (Dan. 12:2). The second judgement will be among the saved, and a decision will be made about who will have a reward and who will not. You may say that you don't care about a reward in heaven, you just want to get there. But I say that when that day comes you will care. When we all stand before God we will give an account of the way we have lived, and all of it will be written in the book. Because what is written is what God has put there through the angels, there will be no argument.

Two things get God's attention, and the first is the fear of God. Do you fear the Lord? I do. You may say that you do not think we are supposed to be afraid of him. But I love him and I am also afraid of him. I have a healthy respect for him; I fear him. One of the first things recorded about the earliest church right after Pentecost was that fear came on every soul (Acts 2:43). The fear of God is almost absent in the church today and it is totally absent in the nation. What is needed is a restoration of the fear of God and it must begin in the church.

The second thing that gets God's attention is the honour that is given to his name. His people love his name. John Newton wrote the words, 'How sweet the name of Jesus sounds in a believer's ear.' And when you love God's name you care about his reputation. The word 'name' refers to influence. You care about what people say; you care about your reputation, your good name. If you love God's name you care about his reputation. You may feel neglected. You may feel no-one is looking after you or interested in you. But all our thoughts are being recorded, all our words and all our deeds.

There are three reasons why this message is so important? One, it shows that God knows those who fear him; he knows those who honour his name. *'The Lord knows those who are his'* (2 Tim. 2:19). This is why believers go straight to heaven without having to be judged first. God has a perfect memory. He knows everything and he knows who are his. Because God sees the end from the beginning, when the judgment does take place God won't learn anything more about us than what he already knows. The book is for our sakes, that we will be able to recall what we have long forgotten. I keep a journal, and when I read it my memory is jogged into remembering things I had forgotten. Nothing is forgotten in God's book.

Two, it is an honour to be recorded in this book because everyone in it is a member of God's family.

Three, the book is important to God. It shows that God notices. It is important that we thank God for the blessings he give us. He hears our thanks and records it.

Three further points need to be made on this verse. God remembers. If you were deeply hurt and you wonder if anybody noticed, God noticed and wrote the hurt down. When you get to heaven you will discover an angel recorded your hurt. He will also write down your reaction to the hurt, noting whether you dignified the trial that God sovereignly brought into your life or whether you murmured or complained. Have you been humiliated? God wrote that down. How did you react to being humiliated? God wrote that down too. All we do and say is being recorded. The thought of God's book of remembrance ought to change our lives.

In the book of Esther, Mordecai found out about a plot to kill the king and told Queen Esther, who in turn told it to the king while giving credit to Mordecai. When the report was investigated and found to be true, two officials were hanged on the gallows. All this was recorded in a book. But Mordecai was not rewarded. But some time later, in the middle of a sleepless night, the King couldn't sleep. He got out that book and noticed that a man by the name of Mordecai had saved his life. When everybody got up the next morning, he asked what had been done for Mordecai. They said that nothing had been done. The king changed that and honoured Mordecai. If a heathen king honoured a man whose deeds were recorded in his book, how much more will God reward those whose names and deeds are in his book of remembrance. By the way, what do you do if you have a sleepless night? Do you watch television or do you read your Bible or pray?

God rewards. And that is why Paul said he was not looking for anything from the Philippians, but he wanted something to be credited to their account. The Philippians, who had sacrificed for Paul and gave of their means to support his ministry, would have that remembered, recorded and rewarded. I wonder which will bring greater joy, the person being rewarded or God doing the rewarding. I think it will mean as much to God as it does to us. Just before Stephen was killed by stoning, he saw the Son of Man standing at the right hand of God (Acts 7:56) although most other references say that he is sitting. Some have put it like this, that Jesus stood to welcome the first martyr home. But I wouldn't be surprised if he stands to welcome all those to whom he says, 'Well done.'

Peter says, 'For it is time for judgment to begin with the family of God; and if it begins with us, what will the outcome be for those who do not obey the gospel of God?' (I Pet. 4:17).

24

HOW GOD SHOWS HIS LOVE

'They will be mine,' says the LORD Almighty, 'in the day when I make up my treasured possession. I will spare them, just as in compassion a man spares his son who serves him. And you will again see the distinction between the righteous and the wicked, between those who serve God and those who do not' (Malachi 3:17-18).

This is a reference to the judgment, the final judgment. A day is coming when every single person who ever lived in this world will be judged. In this verse we see something of the tenderness of God in judgment. In his epistle James writes, you *'have seen the end of the Lord; that the Lord is very pitiful, and of tender mercy'* (Jas. 5:11 AV). I thought of calling this study 'The unashamed God' because he is not going to be ashamed of us at the day of his coming. Jesus is not going to be ashamed to call us brothers and sisters. But I chose the title 'How God shows his love' because the theme of the book of Malachi is *You are loved* even though the people did not feel loved. God's problem was that he didn't feel loved by them.

This passage has much to teach us. Firstly, judgment is coming. All history is moving toward an omega point, a final day of days. Everything that has ever happened in human history is moving towards that great day. Amos and Joel referred to *'the day of the Lord'*, and Jesus referred to it as *'that day'*. Everybody knew exactly what he meant. God sent his Son into the world to prepare us for that day. What preparation have you made for the day of the Lord? Do you realise you are going to stand before God? Those who feared the Lord were remembered and recorded, and a distinction was made between the righteous and the wicked, those who serve God and those who do not.

Secondly, God will be unashamed of those who fear him. Do you fear the Lord? I fear God, though I do not live in continual fear that he is going to get even with me or catch me out, or that he is looking for a chance to punish me. But I respect him; I believe his word. I take very seriously the promise of reward and the warning of the consequence of disobedience. There will be a wonderful moment for those who fear the Lord. But what we discover in this passage is that those who fear the Lord stand out in God's sight.

The people Malachi was addressing were mainly those who asked what was the use of serving God, and concluded that it didn't pay. So the distinction was blurred between the righteous and the wicked, although it seemed that they were all together. However, those who feared the Lord talked with each other and God noticed and he promises one day to unveil who they are. Malachi is telling them that a day is coming when they are going to find that they stood out in the eyes of God, that he noticed them.

God notices whether you dignify trials. He notices whether you forgive those that hurt you. And God notices those who fear him and honour his name. You may feel you are outnumbered and it is not worth it, but God sees, and one day, like a proud parent attending a graduation ceremony, he is going to show how pleased he is with those who feared him. This demonstrates something that has been lost in the modern church, the idea of judgment to come. When was the last time you heard a sermon on the judgment? The Bible says it is appointed to man once to die. Everybody agrees that we are all going to die, but do we really appreciate that the Lord has appointed the very day and time of our deaths. And as it may come unexpectedly we need

to be sure to be ready. Would you be thrilled to your fingertips
if the judgment were to happen in thirty minutes? Would you
panic? Would you fall on your knees and start crying out to God
regardless of what people were thinking? We don't have that
kind of warning, but it is nearer than you think.

Thirdly, this verse shows that in the worst of times God has
a remnant. There was in Malachi's day a professing people of
God, and generally speaking they were rotten to the core. The
Lord saw that. But there was a remnant of people who feared
the Lord; he always had a remnant.

Fourthly, when God says he will spare those who fear him,
that implies that some others will not be spared. Who will he
spare, who will be his on the day he makes up his treasured
possessions? He will spare those who fear him. What about
those who are not spared? God will punish those who are not
spared. The spared are those who were unashamed of the Lord,
who received Jesus Christ as Lord and Saviour. All the others
will be punished. This word is teaching that you will be glad
that day that you served the Lord.

There are three further points. One, there is a promise
implied. God says, 'They will be mine.' God will unveil those
who were faithful. He will show his love for, and pleasure in,
those who were faithful and feared him. He uses this interesting
expression, 'They will be my treasured possession' (3:17) The
Authorised Version says, 'I will come for my jewels'. Psalm 135
uses the expression, 'peculiar treasure' (v. 4 AV). It is impossible
to say who will get greater joy in that day those who are blessed
or God himself as he looks on the faces of those that are his
peculiar treasure. When you give a present, and can see the
look on the face of the person you give it to, you sometimes get
more joy in giving than they do in receiving. It is going to be
like that on the great day when God shows his love for those
who fear him, that love that sent his Son into the world to die
on a cross.

Let me tell you how to prepare for the judgment. You have to recognise that you cannot save yourself by your good works. Being baptised or a church member won't save you. Being born into a Christian home won't save you. Being born into what is still, almost laughably, called a Christian nation won't save you. Doing your best won't save you. Struggling to keep the Ten Commandments, or the sermon on the mount, or the golden rule will not save you. The only way to be saved is by climbing down and admitting you cannot save yourself then putting your whole case in the hands of God, begging him to have mercy because Jesus died for you on the cross. That will save you, and that alone.

Two, the word 'possession'. *'They will be mine'*, God says. He owns them. *'Both the one who makes men holy and those who are made holy are of the same family. So Jesus is not ashamed to call them brothers'* (Heb. 2:11). God will be unashamed to own them and show them off. He will be proud of them. The Bible says that a wise son makes a glad father, and God will be so proud of his own. It may be that you have a broken heart, yet you are saying that although you don't understand, you know God has let it happen for a reason, and you do not question him. If that is the case, one day in front of everybody, God will say, 'Here is my child; he feared me, she honoured my name.' And you will be shown off to everybody because God loves to show his love.

Three, not all are spared. I have already referred to the sacrifices where men offered animals they didn't want anyway. It is like a farmer who told his wife that they had twin calves instead of the single one they were expecting, and that he had decided they should give one of them to the Lord. A week later he came in and said, 'The Lord's calf died today.' 'How do you know which one was the Lord's?' his wife asked. 'I just know it was that one,' her husband told her. There are people like that in the church today. But the sacrificial system was so important because the animals pointed to the one who would be God's lamb, the Lamb. The Old Testament pointed to the Lamb of God that takes away the sin of the world. And it is he that is our hope of getting to heaven.

Four, preservation. I have been using the word 'spared', and the same word appears in Romans 8, probably my favourite chapter in the whole Bible. *'We know that in all things God works for the good of those who love him, who have been called according to his purpose'* and *'He who did not spare his own Son, but gave him up for us all – how will he not also, along with him, graciously give us all things?'* (Rom. 8:28, 32). Those who are spared are spared because God did not spare his Son. When Jesus said, *'For God so loved the world that he gave his one and only Son, that whoever believes in him shall not perish but have eternal life,'* he went on to say, *'God did not send his Son into the world to condemn the world, but to save the world through him'* (John 3:16-17). The assumption was that when God sent his Son into the world, all would be damned; all would be lost. But Jesus' coming into the world is not the reason people will be going to hell. They are already going to hell. God sent his Son into the world not to condemn but to save the world. Some people ask why so many will be lost. The question they ought to ask is why anyone is saved?

25

GOD'S CLASS SYSTEM

And you will again see the distinction between the righteous and the wicked, between those who serve God and those who do not (Malachi 3:18).

The word 'distinction' means seeing a difference between things. It is what differentiates one thing from another. The word 'class' has two definitions in the Oxford Dictionary. One is 'people of the same social or economic level' and the other is 'division according to quality'. Most countries have a class system to some degree. But does God have a class system? Yes, he does, and the classification is quite simple – are you going to heaven or are you going to hell? That is why he talks about the distinction between the righteous and the wicked, between those who serve God and those who do not. Power here below, money, background, education, culture or even intelligence are not important, rather it is whether you are righteous or wicked, saved or lost.

It is interesting that those who serve God are called righteous and those who don't serve God are called wicked. According to this you don't have to be a mass murderer, a wicked criminal or a sex fiend to be called wicked. Wicked is simply the description of those who don't serve God. What does it mean to serve God? A person who serves is someone who does what he or she is told to do.

What does this verse teach us? One, judgment is coming. We are told that God will spare those who honour his name. So those who fear him and honour his name will be spared in the judgment. Two, the distinction between the righteous and the wicked had been blurred for a while. In other words, you can't tell the difference between them. God apparently was hiding his face, not blessing the righteous and not punishing the wicked. But, says Malachi, this blurring of distinction will come to an end. That is the promise. You will again see the distinction between the righteous and the wicked.

Why is this important? Firstly, it shows the striking resemblance of Malachi's day and our own. We are living in a time when the distinction is blurred between the church and the world. It is often hard to tell the difference between Christians and non-Christians. And among those who would call themselves Christians there is almost an absence of the fear of God. People just do what they want to do. Some Christians do today what only the most heinous type of person would have done thirty years ago. Do the things we watch on television bother us? The kind of videos Christian purchase, the kind of magazines they look at, would have horrified believers thirty years ago. But God says that we will again see the distinction between the righteous and the wicked.

Secondly, the relevance between relationship and the final judgment. Revival will be like the final judgement. What will happen at the final judgment? When the Son of Man comes in his glory, all the nations will be gathered before him and he will separate the people from one another as a shepherd separates sheep from goats. He will put the sheep on his right and the goats on his left. (see Matthew 25: 31-46). No distinction? At the judgment it will be obvious who is who.

Jesus told of ten virgins who took their lamps and went out to meet the bridegroom. (see Matthew 25:1-13). Five were foolish; five were wise. The foolish ones took their lamps but did not take oil with them, while the wise took oil. When the bridegroom was a long time coming, all the virgins became drowsy and fell asleep. The distinction was blurred; they all slept. That is the condition of the church today. It is asleep. Think about it. You do not know you are asleep until you wake up. Did you ever lie down and say, 'I am not going to sleep; I am just going to rest?' Then suddenly you waken up and discover you have been asleep. When you sleep, you dream and you do things in your dreams that you wouldn't do while wide awake. Sometimes you can't believe you dreamt about the things you did. Christians today are doing in their spiritual sleep what would horrify them if they were spiritually awake. Another thing about being asleep, we hate the sound of an alarm. Sleeping Christians do not want to hear the alarm call telling them the state they are in. The distinctions are blurred. Now we often cannot tell who are Christian and who are not, but we will be able to tell when Christ comes in reviving power or in judgment.

Compare God's and man's class systems. There are three characteristics of man's class system. First, you are locked into it and there is not a thing you can do about it. Second, it is based on admiration. You get your kicks from somebody saying, 'Oh, is it true that you really know so and so?' Third, it is temporary; it will not last. What about God's class system? First, anybody can be at the top. *The Spirit and the bride say, "Come"'* (Rev. 22:17). That means all who wish to come can come, whoever is thirsty can come and whoever desires to can take the free gift of the water of life. In God's class system you get your thrills from pleasing God. Do you know what it is to please the Lord? Do you know what it is to get that inner testimony that God is happy with you? There is nothing like it. Before you are converted you know that you have displeased him, that your sins have separated you from God. When you are converted, as you serve him you get that feeling of pleasing him. Third, God's class system is permanent; it will not end. *The man who does the will of God lives for ever'* (1 John 2:17). John Newton wrote:

When we've been there ten thousand years,
bright shining as the sun,
we've no less days to sing God's praise
than when we first began.

Jesus said, *'In my Father's house are many rooms; if it were not so, I would have told you. I am going there to prepare a place for you. And if I go and prepare a place for you, I will come again and take you to be with me that you also may be where I am'* (John 14:2-3).

There is dignity in God's class system. God takes you as you are when you come to him in repentance, regardless of what sins you have committed. If you recognise that Jesus took upon himself all your sin, if you catch a glimpse of what the blood of Jesus does for the Father, you will never again be so silly as to think you could be saved by your works, or church membership or baptism, or by turning over a new leaf.

There is nothing but boasting in man's class system, boasting in the kind of clothes you wear, the kind of car you drive and the kind of job you have. Nobody will be boasting in heaven because we will all know we are there because Jesus died for us on the cross. Thank God that in order to be saved you do not have to be born to privilege, you don't require a public school education, you don't need to be cultured and refined. Jesus invited people who laboured and were heavy laden, regardless of where they were in man's class system, to come to him and he would give them rest, and that rest is for eternity. The greatest education you can have just makes you a learned sinner, culture can make you a refined sinner, wealth can make you a rich sinner, but only God can take you and change your life, giving you dignity and a love for him.

Finally, the disclosure of God's class system. Malachi gave the promise that the distinction would again be seen. How will it be seen? It will be seen at the judgment when three things take place. One, you will be summoned. John said, *'I saw a great white throne and him who was seated on it. Earth and sky fled from his presence, and there was no place for them. And I saw the dead, great and small, standing before the throne, and books were opened'* (Rev. 20:11-12). Great and small were there together. Two, there will be separation because Jesus said all the nations will be gathered and he will separate the people one from another as a shepherd separates the sheep from the goats, putting the sheep on his right and the goats on his left (Matt. 25:31-46). Three, there will be surprise. We are told that the righteous will say, *'Lord, when did we see you hungry and feed you, or thirsty and give you something to drink?'* (Matt. 25:37). They will be surprised when Jesus tells them.

The Christian is surprised now. He can hardly believe he's saved because he knows he doesn't deserve it. And at the judgment God will say, 'I came to you and you fed me'. Would you be happy if God's distinction were seen now? What if the Spirit of God came down in great power and we saw it or, better still, what if we heard the sound of the trumpet and were called to stand before God? Are you ready for that great day?

26

WHEN EVIL IS NO MORE

'Surely the day is coming; it will burn like a furnace. All the arrogant and every evildoer will be stubble, and that day that is coming will set them on fire,' says the LORD Almighty. 'Not a root or a branch will be left to them' (Malachi 4:1).

The greatest philosophical theological problem in the world has to do with what we call the origin of evil. Why did God allow evil in the world? It is what gives the atheist the rationale to believe that there is no God. But you don't have to go to Oxford or Harvard to come up with that question. If there is a God, and he is all-powerful and loving, why does he allow things to happen that he could clearly stop? The Bible gives us nothing on the question of the origin of evil, but it gives us everything on how it will end.

There is nobody who could not ask the Lord, 'Why did this happen to me? Or why are there such things as earthquakes, famines, tornadoes and hurricanes?' God doesn't tell us why, and if he did tell us why we wouldn't need faith. He has chosen to bring glory to his name through those who believe his word without the evidence. One day he will clear his name; one day he will explain. I was seventeen when my mother died and what really baffled me was that I thought God had given me a word that she would be healed. After she died, I played the same song over and over again on my record player. And one line of the song was, 'We'll talk it over in the by and by; I'll ask the reason, he'll tell me why.'

Although the Bible does not tell us how evil originated, it does tell us that one day it will come to an end. This verse may seem unattractive because it talks about the Day of Judgment but I am glad to know that there will be a day of judgment. *'Just as man is destined to die once, and after that to face judgment'* (Heb. 9:27). In Malachi 4:1, the prophet is saying what Jesus would say more clearly regarding the nature of eternal punishment. There are many words for eternal punishment, the most common being hell. It is also called a lake of fire, a place of darkness, a place where there will be weeping, wailing and gnashing of teeth. Christians today do not want to believe in hell, they want to focus on the love of God. But although the theme of the book of Malachi is that God's people are loved, here it speaks of judgment. You might ask what kind of love is it that talks about evildoers being stubble set on fire. Malachi here is talking about those who dishonour God's name, and the very fact that he is warning these people about a coming judgment is a sign of the Lord's love.

What does this verse teach us about judgment? It is talking about a day that will be very, very real. And on that day there will be a real distinction between the righteous and the wicked though that distinction is blurred just now. God will punish those who have dishonoured his name, and their punishment will be so thorough that there will not be any opposition. Evil will be no more.

How will that be fulfilled? God can do it in instalments. Take, for example, Saul of Tarsus on the road to Damascus. Saul was not on his way to a prayer group; he was on his way to kill Christians when suddenly he was struck down. In that experience Paul had just a taste of what God can do. There was also a touch of it on the day of Pentecost. Peter spoke with such power that no-one said anything. No-one told him to stop. Instead, they stopped to listen. There was such a spirit of reverence that no-one could voice opposition. God could bring revival at any time and stop the mouths of critics. Malachi may be referring to something like that.

When he speaks to those who dishonour God's name, he tells them that his warning is not the end of the matter, but that there will be a day of judgment when God will remove all competition and render his opponents powerless.

This verse shows us the patience of God. How many of you have wondered why God doesn't answer prayer right away? But just think, this verse was written 2,400 years ago, yet it is still unfulfilled in its ultimate sense. There have been touches of it in human history, but the ultimate fulfilment of this verse is still in the future. This verse is also important because it shows how much God hates sin. *'All the arrogant and every evildoer will be stubble, and that day that is coming will set them on fire.'* It will be such an awful day that no words will describe it. Another reason this is important is that we who are alive can still hear Malachi's warning and decide whose side we are going to be on.

Malachi refers to what Jesus made clear regarding eternal punishment. Jesus said, *'If your hand causes you to sin, cut it off. It is better for you to enter life maimed than with two hands to go into hell, where the fire never goes out. And if your foot causes you to sin, cut it off...'* (Mark 9:43-45). The Lord is not talking about literally cutting off your foot or cutting off your hand. What he means is that if your foot offends you, if you walk to a place where you don't bring honour and glory to God, stop going there rather than continuing to sin and ending up in hell where the fire never goes out. And the same with what you do with you hands or see with your eyes.

Could it be that Malachi is talking about what Jesus referred to as hell? That is possible. Could it be the fire that Paul writes about? *'His work will be shown for what it is, because the Day will bring it to light. It will be revealed with fire, and the fire will test the quality of each man's work'* (1 Cor. 3:13). Fire will test the quality of each man's work. If what he has built survives he will receive a reward; if it is burnt up he will suffer loss. He himself will be saved but only as one escaping through the flames. I mention this because Malachi talks about a furnace, he talks about fire, and I wonder if this could be the fire that Paul is referring to, if they are both speaking about saved people who will go to heaven but have no reward. Be grateful that day is in the future and we can still do something about it. To scoff at this reflects what Peter calls wilful ignorance.

What kind of fire is meant? It could mean material fire, literal fire, supernatural fire, or it could be metaphorical fire. Or it could be all three or maybe two of the three. God's word says that the day is coming, that will burn like a furnace, and that all the arrogant and evil doers will be stubble. The day that is coming will set them on fire.

Firstly, material fire. One scholar writing on this verse put it like this, 'The day will be one of tropical heat, when parched vegetation suddenly catches fire and dry fields become one vast oven in which even the roots of the plants are reduced to ash.' This supposes that the fire will be a natural phenomena. Some think this refers to the rising heat caused be the reduction in the ozone layer. Others think it could refer to nuclear war.

Secondly, metaphysical or supernatural fire. Moses' burning bush is an example of this. He saw a bush on fire that didn't burn up because it was burning with supernatural fire. Hell is supernatural fire, which is why Jesus could say, '... *their worm does not die, and the fire is not quenched'* (Mark 9:48). It is not ordinary fire. The question is often asked if this verse could mean annihilation. This is the view that everything is burned up and nothing exists as though it had never been. Annihilation is the teaching that everything is gone as though it never was. Malachi makes sure we can't believe that because he says every evildoer will be stubble. If it were annihilation there would be no stubble left. The use of the word stubble makes me think that we are probably talking about metaphorical fire. It may be a figure of speech to teach us that when God rolls up his sleeves in judgment, the arrogant and the evildoers will no longer be a threat. They will just be stubble. In other words, they will be inoperative; they will have no power to influence; they will be completely and utterly helpless.

Those are the possibilities, but what we know is that God is going to work in such a way that evildoers know hell. They will be put to shame. That also rules out annihilation. If they ceased to be, they could not be ashamed. Adolf Hitler will be ashamed, Mussolini and Stalin will be ashamed and, if you are an unbeliever, he will make sure you are ashamed too. God gives you warning after warning and you think you can still get off with unbelief. But don't think that will last for ever. One day God will say that enough is enough. And part of your punishment will be having to live with yourself knowing how foolish, how stupid you have been.

Richard Bewes said, 'The difference between the Christian faith and all other religions is a four letter word. With every religion it always is do, do, do. With the Christian faith it is done; it is done.' Just before Jesus died, he said, *'It is finished'* (John 19:30). He paid your debt; it is done. God invites you to come to him so that in advance of that day you know that, whatever kind of fire there is, you will not be burned to stubble. God shall wipe away all tears from the eyes of those who come to him. For them there will be no more death nor crying nor pain (Rev. 21:4). There will be no Satan to accuse them. He will be out of the picture.

One last point, the fires of hell never satisfy the justice of God. That is one of the reasons hell is eternal. But although the fire never satisfies him, one drop of the blood of Jesus does. And it is through his blood that God's people are spared from the eternal fire.

27

THE FIRE OF GOD

'Surely the day is coming; it will burn like a furnace. All the arrogant and every evildoer will be stubble, and that day that is coming will set them on fire,' says the LORD Almighty. 'Not a root or a branch will be left to them' (Malachi 4:1).

Malachi talks about fire, and Peter writes about it. *'The day of the Lord will come like a thief. The heavens will disappear with a roar; the elements will be destroyed by fire, and the earth and everything in it will be laid bare'* (2 Pet. 3:10). Peter says that this will happen on the day of the Lord's coming; that that day will bring about the destruction of the heavens by fire and the elements will melt in the heat. What is that day? It is the day of the Second Coming of Jesus. Jesus first came 2,000 years ago to die on a cross to bear the penalty of our sins. His second coming will be very different. *'When the Lord Jesus is revealed from heaven in blazing fire with his powerful angels'* (2 Thes. 1:7). That's wonderfully different!

It is interesting that Malachi's prophecy cannot be fully understood until either it is further explained or it comes to fulfilment. For example, Isaiah said, *'He was despised and rejected by men, a man of sorrows, and familiar with suffering. Like one from whom men hide their faces he was despised, and we esteemed him not'* (Is. 53:3). People wondered who and what he was talking about? He went on to say, *'Surely he took up our infirmities and carried our sorrows, yet we considered him stricken by God, smitten by him, and afflicted … We all, like* sheep, have gone astray, each of us has turned to his own way; and the LORD has laid on him the iniquities of us all' (Is. 53:4,6). But it was only when Jesus died on the cross and the Spirit came down that people looked at Isaiah 53 and really knew what it was about. He was describing Jesus hundreds of years in advance.

Malachi is also describing the future when he says that the day is coming and that it will burn like a furnace. We have already discussed the different kinds of fire, but there is still more to say on the subject. Moses saw a literal, though supernatural, fire when the bush burned but was not consumed. On Mount Sinai, just before God gave the Ten Commandments, there was fire. 'Mount Sinai was covered with smoke, because the LORD descended on it in fire. The smoke billowed up from it like smoke from a furnace, the whole mountain trembled violently' (Ex. 19:18). That was supernatural fire. Later the children of Israel were guided by fire at night and a cloud by day (Ex. 40:36). These were supernatural fires. Then we read that, 'Moses and Aaron then went into the Tent of Meeting. When they came out, they blessed the people; and the glory of the LORD appeared to all the people. Fire came out from the presence of the LORD and consumed the burnt offering and the fat portions on the altar. And when all the people saw it, they shouted for joy and fell face down' (Lev. 9:23-24). Here God used supernatural fire to show his power.

On other occasions fire is used as a figure of speech. Jeremiah said, '"Is not my word like a fire," declares the LORD, "and like a hammer that breaks a rock in pieces?' (Jer. 23:29). He also said that he had fire in his bones, he was so full of the message. When John the Baptist came, people asked if he was the one that should come, or would there be another. He told them that he was not the one, but that 'One more powerful than I will come, the thongs of whose sandals I am not worthy to untie. He will baptise you with the Holy Spirit and with fire' (Luke 3:16). He was referring to the supernatural fire of God.

Which kind of fire will you experience? It is not a question of whether you are going to experience fire at all, because everybody will experience some kind of fire. You can submit to God and know the fire John Wesley described when he felt his heart warmed by the Holy Spirit. That is what was happening in Leviticus when the fire came down and consumed the sacrifice. When you put your trust in the sacrificed blood of Jesus, the Spirit will come down and testify in order that you know all of your sins are forgiven. And the day is coming when we will have to stand before God and give an account of our lives. You will be there and I will be there; it is called the Day of Days, it is called the Day of the Lord. And according to the apostle Paul it will be revealed with fire. That fire will consume all your bad works if your trust is in Jesus. The extra baggage that you have accumulated along the way will be consumed because nothing unclean can enter into heaven.

The fire of God is, however, also referred to as an everlasting fire, and this is something I can't wholly take in or understand. God's word says, with reference to the person who rejects all the warnings of the Bible, *'He will be tormented with burning sulphur in the presence of the holy angels and of the Lamb. And the smoke of their torment rises for ever and ever. There is no rest day or night for those who worship the beast and his image, or for anyone who receives the mark of his name'* (Rev. 14:10-11). My own view is that the fire referred to here is supernatural fire from which those who are condemned cannot escape. But we are told we do not have to have a part of this if in our hearts we admit that we have sinned against God and go to him confessing our sins and asking him to wash them all away in the blood of Jesus. If we do that, he washes away all our sins and the fire will come down to cleanse us.

Sometimes the fire can be referred to as a figure of speech. For example, Isaiah says, *'When you walk through the fire , you will not be burned; the flames will not set you ablaze'* (Is. 43:2).

Isaiah is not talking about supernatural fire in that case, and he is not talking about literal fire. We sometimes talk about a major trial as fire, about suffering as fire. And the Bible refers to the fires of God's chastening. If you are a Christian, and you are going through these fires, it is because God is chastening you. Scripture tells us that the Lord chastens/disciplines those he loves. In order to get your attention he puts you through the fire. If you are going through the fire, and you are not a Christian, all I can say is that God is on your case; he is trying to get your attention and you had better pay heed to his warning.

Four further points on the fire of God. One, God's fire is a jealous fire. The God of the Bible is jealous. And God is up-front about his jealousy though most people would deny theirs. Jealousy is not a good human quality. But although we don't want to admit to being jealous, God tells us quite openly that he is jealous. He makes no secret of it. *'The LORD your God is a consuming fire, a jealous God'* (Deut. 4:24). *'I, the LORD your God, am a jealous God'* (Deut. 5:9). You talk about a jealous lover, but you haven't seen anything compared to God's jealous love for you. And when you go off the rails, God has a way of saying, 'I am not going to allow that kind of lifestyle. I don't like it. I am a holy God; I am a jealous God and I won't have it.' If you have gone off the rails and met God's jealousy, remember that it is a sign of his love for you.

Two, the fire of God is a judgmental fire. In Noah's day the Lord used water to punish the world, but on the day that is coming, says Malachi, Paul and Peter, the whole world will see the fire of God. You are going to see it and it will be judgment. Malachi says that day is coming and it will burn like a furnace in which all the arrogant and evildoers will be reduced to stubble. What does this mean? Think of those who have a high profile in this world, the Saddam Husseins and Joseph Stalins who caused much suffering and of whom people were afraid. And think of the suffering you have caused other people. God says to them and to you, if you are not saved through the blood of Jesus, one day you will be as stubble. You will stand before him and the fire of his judgment will make you as stubble.

Three, God's fire is a judicious fire, it is carried out with wisdom. God's judgment is wise, astute and prudent. In this life you have a touch of that fire and its suffering during times of being disciplined, when God gives you a slap on the wrist, or when he puts you flat on your back. He may take your job from you, or your health or your money. Why does he do that? He does it to discipline, to get our attention. *'Why should any living man complain when punished for his sins?'* (Lam. 3:39).

If God is doing that to you, you should be thankful and heed his warnings. In other words, if in this life God won't let you get away with this or that while other people seem to get away with the same things, it is God who is disciplining you, and he disciplines those he loves. Many years ago, when we were first living in Florida (we are now retired here), we had a most beautiful orchid tree in the front garden. One day our son TR and his little friend Billy, who lived next door, decided that the tree needed some trimming. I let Billy go home but I had to deal with our son. TR asked why he was being disciplined when Billy was not. I told him that it was because Billy was not our son, and he was. When God disciplines you it is a sign that you are special.

Four, God's fire is a just fire; it is fair. It is the arrogant and evildoers who will be stubble.

28

JUST HEALING

But for you who revere my name, the sun of righteousness will rise with healing in its wings. And you will go out and leap like calves released from the stall (Malachi 4:2).

Here we have God's authentic ministry of healing, and when God heals his healing is just. That means it will bring honour and glory to his name. There are those who think you can make God do anything you want, make him heal whoever you choose. But what I know to be true is that, were he willing, he could bestow on us a healing presence. Healing is a sovereign manifestation of God's glory. In the New Testament God healed people, Jesus healed many, many people. Why? He healed them because he loves people, and he takes no pleasure in anybody being in pain. If you are in pain, God takes no pleasure in that. I don't know why God sometimes withholds mercy, but one day he will explain what he meant by those words *'my ways are higher than your ways'.*

Another reason God healed through Jesus is that he wanted to authenticate the ministry of his Son. It was a way of putting a seal on Jesus. And the authentication continued after Jesus died on the cross, rose from the dead and went to heaven, because the healing didn't stop. It continued in the early church. *'Is any one of you sick? He should call the elders of the church to pray over him and anoint him with oil in the name of the Lord. And the prayer offered in faith will make the sick person well; the*

Lord will raise him up' (Jam. 5:14-15). I have longed for that to
happen in my own church because it authenticated the ministry
of Jesus, it authenticated the early church and it is a testimony
to the power of Christ. However, it is not the main thing. The
main thing is to be saved, the main thing is to know that if you
were to die today you would go to heaven, which is a much
better healing. In heaven no healing will be necessary. In heaven
there will be no crying, no pain and no tears. Everyone there
will be totally and completely healed.

What does this verse say? First, it encouraged the small
minority of those who revered God's name. They were surrounded
by people who dishonoured God in their sacrifices, their
marriages and their attitudes. Second, it showed that God
noticed those who revered his name. God hates complaining;
he hates murmuring. But he loves to hear his name revered.
God sees those who take their suffering and disability with
dignity, who forgive those who hurt or abuse them. God knows
where you are; he knows your thoughts. Third, this verse is
there because these people were hurting. This small minority of
people were hurting. It is not fun to be a minority; it is not fun
to be outnumbered. It is a lot easier to be like everybody else.
But these people were different because they revered God, and
their hurting got God's attention.

Why is this message important? One, because God knows
who needs healing. That healing may be physical healing or it
may be healing because you need closure in a certain situation.
Maybe you didn't say 'goodbye' to your father before he died;
maybe you didn't say 'I am sorry' to someone; maybe there are
open wounds as far as your heart is concerned. God knows your
need of healing. Two, because you need to know that God has
been in the healing business for a long time. It is not something
that first emerged in the New Testament. He knows what he is
doing. He is the one that made us; he knows us through and
through. And God, who knows who needs healing, is in the

healing business. Three, this is important because God wants to reward those who revere him in desperate conditions. He knows you are outnumbered, and he says that if you revere his name the Sun of Righteousness will rise with healing.

Four more points need to be made. One, the promise of healing. Do you know the first time healing must have taken place in the Bible? It was when God closed up Adam's side. Then in Genesis 20:17, Abraham prayed to God and God healed Abimelech. And one of the best known verses in the Bible is about healing. *'If my people, who are called by my name, will humble themselves and pray and seek my face and turn from their wicked ways, then will I hear from heaven and will forgive their sin and will heal their land'* (2 Chron. 7:14). Elijah's prophetic ministry was paralleled by healing, as was the ministry of Elisha. God heals throughout the Bible and beyond. You may say that you don't have faith that you will be healed. You are not required to have faith; all you are required to do is ask for prayer. There is no Bible verse that rebukes you for not having enough faith to be healed. If any are rebuked it is those who do the praying, that they do not have faith. God will honour the fact that you ask to be prayed for.

Two, the purpose of healing. The purpose of healing is to relieve pain. I am looking forward to going to heaven because we will all be perfectly healed there, and there will be no more pain.

Three, to rebuke scoffers. In the gospels Jesus healed to rebuke scoffers and, in the Book of Acts, God healed to rebuke scoffers. He has a way of putting people in their place. Healing will not cause people to become Christians, but God can use it to rebuke those who scoff at the faith

Four, the ultimate purpose of healing is to vindicate God, and that is when it is just healing. If God heals you it will be because he wants you to be free from pain, he wants to give you a taste of heaven to come. But the ultimate reason for your healing will be to vindicate his name.

Notice who are healed – *'you who revere my name'* (4:3). That does not mean that they are the only ones to be healed. God says he will have mercy on whom he will have mercy and he will be gracious to whom he will be gracious. Sometimes God heals people just to be gracious to them. They didn't deserve it, they didn't revere God's name, he just did it. However the promise is given to the people who revere his name.

There are three things that get God's attention. Firstly, if you love his word you touch his heart. That means you want to know the Bible really well because you want to know him, and the better you know the Bible the better you know him. *"Thou hast magnified thy word above all thy name* (Ps. 138:2 AV). Secondly, when you love the blood of Jesus. What touches God's heart quicker than anything else is when you appeal to the blood of Jesus. God has never forgotten the sight of his Son dying on a cross; he has never forgotten the blood that satisfied his justice once for all. And all who point to the blood of Jesus get God's attention. Thirdly, when you revere his name. His name refers to his reputation, his authority. It is summed up in a five letter word, 'Jesus'. 'How sweet the name of Jesus sounds in a believer's ear.' The promise is to you if you revere his name. Fourthly, the preciousness of being healed. To be with somebody who has been healed is infinitely precious. And the person who does the healing is the Sun of Righteousness.

29

THE SUN OF RIGHTEOUSNESS

But for you who revere my name, the sun of righteousness will rise with healing in its wings. And you will go out and leap like calves released from the stall (Malachi 4:2).

This is one of the occasions in the Old Testament when Jesus is referred to without using his name. It was only later that people realized it spoke of Jesus. Here we have the last Old Testament reference to Jesus, and he is called Sun of Righteousness. The last reference to him in the New Testament is, *'I, Jesus, have sent my angel to give you this testimony for the churches. I am the Root and the Offspring of David, and the bright Morning Star'* (Rev. 22:16). Isn't it interesting that the last reference to Jesus in the Old Testament is Sun of Righteousness and the last reference to him in the New Testament the Bright Morning Star.

Although in the Old Testament you don't find the name Jesus, what you do have is Jesus being described in such a way that once you have received him as your Lord and Saviour, and you begin to read the Bible under the Holy Spirit's guidance, you discover that it is referring to Jesus. It amazes you how you could have missed it, but you can't see it until the Holy Spirit reveals it to you. The Bible is not a book like history or psychology or philosophy or architecture. It is a spiritual book written by holy men of old moved by the Spirit. And the only way we can understand the Bible is to have the same Holy Spirit in our hearts that God used to write the Bible all those years ago.

The first time Jesus is referred to is in Genesis chapter 3:15, when God says, *'I will put enmity between you and the woman, and between your offspring and hers; he will crush your head, and you will strike his heel.'* That is the first promise of Jesus in the Bible. In Leviticus Jesus emerges as our Passover Lamb. In Ruth he comes forward as our kinsman redeemer. The Psalms show him as our shepherd. In Proverbs he is our wisdom. Song of Solomon has him as the rose of Sharon, the lily of the valleys. The book of Daniel reveals Jesus as the Son of Man.

This verse contains a promise of healing for those who revere God's name. The people to whom this promise was given had been going through the most difficult time of their lives, and the promise was that the Sun of Righteousness would come in the darkest hour, and that he would bring healing, justice and fairness. If you are in a situation from which you feel you cannot escape, remember the greatest promise of the Bible, next to the promises of Jesus. *'We know that in all things God works for the good of those who love him, who have been called according to his purpose'* (Rom. 8:28).

That promise is in the present tense. It is not, therefore, a promise to those who once loved God but now are off the rails, rather it is a promise to those who realise they have wandered, and who have finished with what brought them down. It is for those who say no to all that displeases God and who love him now, in the present tense. If that is where you are, the promise is for you regardless of what you have been through. Whatever has happened, whatever is in the past, whatever haunts you, God will make it all work together for good, so good that you wouldn't take anything in the world but what happened.

When the sun rises in the morning, it marks the end of the night. And the coming of the Sun of Righteousness marks the end of an era. He is the Bright Morning Star. He is that bright star at the end of the night as the sun rises that let's you know that good things are coming with the dawn of a new day.

Why is this important? First, it shows how people in the Old Testament looked forward to Jesus. Second, it shows that God knows how much we can bear. This was addressed to people who revered the name of the Lord but suffered a lot. Third, it shows how God steps in without our effort. We are incapable of making the sun rise. It is out of our hands; it is something God does. Are you the type of person who tries to make things happen? Are you always living in the fast lane? And are you so tired of that lifestyle that you now want to see what God can do? If that is you, you need to recognise that God can do for you what you cannot do for yourself. That is why he sent his Son to be a Saviour, to be the Sun of Righteousness and to come with healing.

The title Sun of Righteousness shows the power of Jesus. The sun means light. When the sun rises it illuminates. Jesus said that he is the light of the world. The sun gives heat to warm the earth. The temperature is lower in the morning; it is when the sun rises that it begins to warm up. As God will give you light for your mind, he will also give you warmth for your cold heart. Has anybody told you that you don't have a heart? Has anybody told you that you are so cold and distant that people can't reach you? If they have, Jesus can warm your heart. When John Wesley, the founder of Methodism, described his conversion, he said that he found his heart strangely warmed. The sun also gives energy. And in the same way that we get our energy from the sun, God will renew our will. If you have lost heart and lost motivation, the Sun of Righteousness will come with healing and renew your will. But he comes on two conditions. One, you love him. Two, you revere his name.

There are three further points in this verse. Firstly, it refers to the excellence of his name. God chose the best of his creation, the sun that gives light to the world, to describe Jesus. Now we are told in Hebrews 1:3-4 that Jesus *'is the radiance of God's glory and the exact representation of his being, sustaining all things by his powerful word. After he had provided purification for sins, he sat down at the right hand of the Majesty in heaven. So he became as much superior to the angels as the name he has inherited is superior to theirs.'* There is power in the name of Jesus. John Newton's great hymn, 'How sweet the name of Jesus sounds in a believer's ear' shows the excellence of his name.

Secondly, it means the end of the night. The sanctified minority that suffered was outnumbered by those who wanted to trade in their wives for exotic young foreign women. They lived among people who had forgotten God's laws and who behaved as they pleased, while complaining about the Lord without realising that he heard their complaints. And God comes to that minority and says, 'To you who revere my name I come with healing.' Has life seemed like a long night for you, and do you think that the morning will never come? If it has, this word prophesies the end of the night.

Thirdly, it shows that something new is coming, that justice is coming at last. God knows the next step forward and things will start to happen if you keep your eyes upon Jesus. Things will turn around and you will discover that it really did work together for good. God is faithful, an unchanging God, and he comes with justice and healing.

God loves to do the new and the different. Are you ready for the new and different? God says that it is morning; the Sun has risen and the end of the nightmare has come.

30

JUST FREE

'But for you who revere my name, the sun of righteousness will rise with healing in its wings. And you will go out and leap like calves released from the stall. Then you will trample down the wicked; they will be ashes under the soles of your feet on the day when I do these things, says the Lord Almighty (Malachi 4:2-3).

In these lines Malachi is prophesying a day when Israel's long national nightmare would be over. However, only those who had revered God's name would benefit from this. It is a word to the sanctified minority. Malachi is prophesying a day when the underdog would be the top dog. No one enjoys being the underdog and God knows that. There is a very interesting prophecy in the book of Deuteronomy. *'The Lord will make you the head, not the tail. If you pay attention to the commands of the Lord your God that I give you this day and carefully follow them, you will always be at the top, never at the bottom'* (Deut. 28:13). It may be that you are the underdog, you are in a minority, you feel as though you are nothing. If so, this verse is for you.

These people were affected by the state of the nation even though they revered the Lord. But the Lord knows those that are his and he sent Malachi to tell them that a day would come when God would give them indescribable joy. *'You will go out and leap like calves released from the stall.'* These oppressed people had been penned in, now they were to be free. When penned animals are loosed, they are so excited they don't know what to do with themselves.

Why is this such an important word? Firstly, it is an apt description of conversion.

> Amazing grace, how sweet the sound,
> that saved a wretch like me;
> I once was lost but now am found,
> was blind but now I see.

John Newton wrote these words to describe what it is like to be saved. I was brought up in the hills of Kentucky right at the end of the Cane Ridge Revival, what American historians call America's Second Awakening. Then you grew up knowing that when you died you would go either to heaven or to hell. And when people were converted in those days they were so excited because they knew that we must all stand before the judgement seat of Christ and give an account of the deeds done in the body. They were so excited! They were like calves leaping, released from a stall. They just about went wild, they shouted and yelled and screamed with joy. They said it was like the sound of Niagara, thousands of people all at once, and all because they knew they weren't going to go to hell. I will never forget when God graciously gave me what I call full assurance. It was the most wonderful feeling to know that I couldn't be lost, that I would never be in hell. That is why this verse is such an apt description of conversion.

Secondly, it shows the relief and the joy of vindication. To be vindicated means to be free from blame. We all want to have a good name. *'A good name is more desirable than great riches; to be esteemed is better than silver or gold'* (Pro. 22:1). These people were unvindicated; they were feeling horrible. And they were beginning to wonder if God cared. They had not sacrificed diseased animals, or divorced their wives. And Malachi prophecies the day when they will trample down the wicked. They will be ashes under their feet on the day when God does these things.

Thirdly, it describes the immediate feeling of freedom after a long era of bondage. The moment you hear the good news, or the moment you are set free, you just go wild. You are so excited, so thrilled to be free. There is nothing like it in the world. When Nelson Mandela was released after having been in prison for twenty-six years, he didn't run like a wild calf, rather he moved in a stately walk. I found myself weeping at what must be going on in that man's mind. And I will never forget Trevor McDonald, the television newsreader. He was so excited; he was the one who was like a calf being released. It was amazing to hear his voice. If your spirit is in bondage ask God to set you free. Then you can have the thrill of real freedom.

Fourthly, it shows how God turns on the oppressor then directs the oppressed to participate in revenge. *'Then you will trample down the wicked; they will be ashes under the soles of your feet on the day when I do these things'* (4:3). Revelation 3:9 says, *'I will make those who are of the synagogue of Satan, who claim to be Jews though they are not, but are liars – I will make them come and fall down at your feet and acknowledge that I have loved you.'*

Joseph, in the Old Testament, experienced that when his brothers had to bow before him and recognise that God loved Joseph and had chosen him specially. But it was because Joseph had already forgiven them in his heart that he could be trusted with that kind of vindication. When God does this, it is not to allow the person who has been oppressed to get all the anger out of his system, far from it. God's vindication is to bring him glory. But his word teaches our part in that vindication. *'Do you not know that the saints will judge the world? And if you are to judge the world, are you not competent to judge trivial cases? Do you not know that we will judge angels?'* (I Cor. 6:2). And this is what we have in the book of Malachi. The day will come when those who have been most cruel to you will be judged by you.

There are three degrees of freedom. One, the freedom that comes by being saved. It is called justification by faith. That means being declared righteous simply because you believe that Jesus died on the cross for your sins. It happens when you come to the place where you transfer the trust that you had in your good works to Christ, and rely upon what Jesus did for you on the cross. Because of your faith in the blood of Jesus, God puts to your credit a righteousness equal to the righteousness of Christ so that you will not be judged by your works when you stand before him. Rather you will be judged by the righteousness of Jesus. The result of that transaction is wonderful freedom. Paul says, *'It is for freedom that Christ has set us free. Stand firm, then, and do not let yourselves be burdened again by a yoke of slavery'* (Gal. 5:1).

Two, the freedom that comes from the renewal of the Holy Spirit. For some this seems like being saved all over again. For others it may come when they begin to find out how real God is and when they discover that his word is really, really true. That is when the Bible comes alive.

Three, the freedom that comes from glorification. This freedom is only enjoyed after you die and go to heaven or when Jesus comes again. And it involves being free from the devil, never again having him tempt you, never again fighting that awful feeling, never again worrying about being up one day and down the next. That will all be over. Then you will be free from pain, from suffering and from tears. What freedom!

The freedom described by Malachi is that which is prior to going to heaven. There comes a time when God says that enough is enough and he decides to vindicate that sanctified minority. Perhaps you are longing for the day when God will clear your name. But this comes on the condition that you have done nothing to cause your bad name, his bad reputation, because the kind of vindication he brings is one in which he gets all the glory.

There are five other points on these verses. First, a description of relief. The Lord says, *'You will go out and leap like calves released from the stall.'* Do you remember when the Berlin Wall fell? It started out with a handful of dust falling, but in just a matter of hours nobody could stop it. Before long bulldozers were hauling it down. What relief was on the faces of those who were there when the wall came down. But that is nothing to the relief of being free from the guilt of sin through Jesus Christ.

Second, a description of release. You will go out and leap like calves released from the stall. The worst bondage in the world is the bondage of the law, the bondage of legalism. For others it is the opposite extreme, the bondage of a habit that they cannot break. God wants you to be free. If the Son makes you free you will be free indeed. Where the Spirit of the Lord is, there is liberty, and if you know in your heart you are in bondage go to him for release.

Third, a description of revenge. *'Then you will trample down the wicked; they will be ashes under the soles of your feet on the day when I do these things'* (4:3). When we take revenge it always backfires. God says that is not how it has to be done. We have to let him do it. When he does it, it is not personal, though he lets us participate in it.

Fourth, a description of respect. The sanctified minority were promised that the day would come when they would be respected. We have seen that in Revelation 3:9. *'Do not take revenge, my friends, but leave room for God's wrath, for it is written: "It is mine to avenge; I will repay," says the Lord'* (Rom. 12:19). God will make them come and fall down at your feet and acknowledge that he has loved you. And God will enable you to live in such a way that you will get a sense of self-esteem. He does not want you to go around with an inferiority complex. Rather we should have a confidence that is based on our relationship with God.

Fifth, a description of reward. It comes down to this, God is going to reward those who didn't go with the trend. Jesus said,

'He who receives you receives me, and he who receives me receives the one who sent me. Anyone who receives a prophet because he is a prophet will receive a prophet's reward, and anyone who receives a righteous man because he is a righteous man will receive a righteous man's reward. And if anyone gives even a cup of cold water to one of these little ones because he is my disciple, I tell you the truth, he will certainly not lose his reward' (Matt. 10:40-42).

There is a golden thread running right through the Bible. Imagine I had a strong needle with a golden thread and I took that needle and stuck it through the Bible and pulled it out the other side so that any time you opened a page you would see that gold thread. The gold thread is that God vindicates and rewards; he clears the name of those that have been hurt as long as they let him do it, and he will reward them for waiting. Your day will come and, when it does, you will be like those calves set free, running and jumping with delight.

31

WHY REMEMBER GOD'S LAW?

Remember the law of my servant Moses, the decrees and laws I gave him at Horeb for all Israel (Malachi 4:4).

Just before he finishes, it is as though God says through Malachi, 'Oh, by the way, remember the law of my servant Moses, the decrees and law I gave him for all Israel.' 400 years later Jesus came to earth, and early in his ministry he preached what we now call the Sermon on the Mount. He said, *'Do not think that I have come to abolish the Law or the Prophets; I have not come to abolish them but to fulfil them'* (Matt. 5:17). Why did he say that? It was because the Pharisees, who were members of a kind of religious political party in Israel, thought he was going to do away with the law. Then there were the Zealots, some of whom hoped he would do away with the Law and start all over again. That made the Pharisees suspicious of what Jesus was teaching. That is why Jesus made this statement, adding, *'I tell you the truth, until heaven and earth disappear, not the smallest letter, not the least stroke of a pen, will by any means disappear from the Law until everything is accomplished'* (Matt. 5:18). The last prophet of the Old Testament, just before he ends his prophecy, teaches that the Law should be remembered.

Although there was a sanctified minority, generally speaking the Law was just head knowledge to the Israelites. They did not have it in their hearts. Here it is as though Malachi is telling those who did revere God's name that they should remember

God's Law, the fulfilment of which they were waiting. They had the promise and they had to hang on to it, knowing that it would be fulfilled one day.

To transpose that to our situation, if you are waiting for something to happen that hasn't happened, and God has given you a word, he has given you a promise. Remember God's word. Saturate yourself in the Bible while you wait. Do you have a Bible reading plan? How much do you read your Bible? How much do you pray? Malachi says, *'Remember the law.'*

Moses law was still in force when Malachi was alive. It was not at the end of its usefulness, nor will it ever be at the end of its usefulness. Martin Luther, who rediscovered the teaching of justification by faith, said that if you can understand the law and gospel you will be a good theologian. Later he said that there is not a person alive who understands the contrasts between the law and the gospel. And he was a theologian steeped in God's word.

This verse is a warning to that sanctified minority not to take the word of God for granted. And we need to hear that too. We need to remember God's word while we wait for him to come. We too need to hear the warning as we wait for the glory.

The law was still in its parenthetical period in Malachi's day. Romans 5:20 says, *'The law was added'*, and Galatians 3:19, enlightens us regarding the purpose of the law. *'What, then, was the purpose of the law? It was added because of transgressions until the Seed to whom the promise referred had come...'* The law was, therefore, a 1,300 year long parenthesis – like brackets in a sentence – which ended when Jesus died on the cross. It was intended as a temporary measure in God's plan.

Why then should we remember God's law, especially now that Christ has perfectly fulfilled it. Jesus said, *'Do not think that I have come to abolish the Law or the Prophets; I have not come to abolish them but to fulfil them'* (Matt. 5:17). Paul says that we are not under the law. *'Now that faith has come, we are no longer under the supervision of the law* (Gal. 3:25), and, *'If you are led by the Spirit, you are not under the law'* (Gal. 5:18). Sadly many Christians don't even know what the law of Moses is!

The law, which is in three parts, was given around 1300 BC. The three are: the moral law (the Ten Commandments), the civil law (how the people of Israel were to be governed) and the ceremonial law (how God was to be worshipped). It is this three-part law that Malachi refers to when he says, *'Remember the law of my servant Moses, the decrees and laws I gave him at Horeb for all Israel'* (4:4). Many Christians are confused over the relationship between the gospel and the law, some wrongly imagining that freedom from the law means that people can live as they please. This is called Antinomianism, literally 'against law'.

What was the original purpose of the law? It was given to restrain from sin through fear of punishment. But it also revealed sin by showing what displeased God. It further showed the righteousness God requires of his people. That standard is the same whether living under the ancient law or walking by the Spirit.

The law, however, was a temporary measure, finding its complete fulfilment in Jesus' sinless life and perfect sacrificial, substitutionary death. And yet, if we opt to live under the law that Jesus fulfilled on our behalf, it will accuse us and make us legalistic. But if we walk in the Spirit, we will not only manifest the external righteousness that the law requires, but the inner righteousness (love, joy, peace etc.) that the law cannot produce. If we walk in the Spirit we are not under the law, yet, paradoxically, we fulfil it. Try to walk by the law and you will come short. Live by the Spirit, and you have it both ways! Furthermore, under the law there is no assurance of salvation, rather there is unprofitable introspection and, at worst, despair.

Why then should we, who are not living in Malachi's day but under the gospel of Jesus Christ, remember the law? Firstly, it is a big part of God's infallible word. Most of the Old Testament was written during this parenthetical period, and knowing that helps us to understand some difficult passages. Also much of the New Testament has to do with the law. Paul labours to show that we are not under it in Christ, but we need to grasp the law to know what it is we are not under – or many of his epistles will make little sense. Although we are not under the law, Paul endorses its right use. *'We know that the law is good if one uses it properly'* (I Tim. 1:8).

Secondly, the righteousness of the law is unchanging. Everything that is prohibited in the Old Testament is equally prohibited by the Spirit's application of the gospel. Idolatry, the misuse of God's name, adultery, murder, stealing etc. are sins that the Holy Spirit will not abide. In fact, if someone embraced the gospel by the Spirit's effectual calling, and obediently walked in the Spirit, he would keep the righteousness of the law even if he had never heard of the Ten Commandments! That is how pure the Holy Spirit is, and how constant his standards are. We need to remember the law because it serves as a backdrop to verify whether we are truly walking in the Spirit. If we claim to be walking in the Spirit, and are living in adultery, or engaged in theft etc., that claim has to be rejected. The Holy Spirit was not given to us to replace the law; rather it is with his help that we use it as a check-list to show us how truly we are walking with him.

Thirdly, the law shows us what Jesus had to do to save us. The law has never, ever, been fulfilled by anyone other than Jesus. His promise to fulfil the law (Matt. 5:17) was, according to Dr Martyn Lloyd-Jones, the most extraordinary and stupendous claim he ever made! But he did it in full. When Jesus uttered these glorious words, *'It is finished'* (John 19:30), he used a colloquial expression from the ancient market place, and it meant 'paid in full'. The law demanded to be fully fulfilled, and no-one else could do it. That yoke, which the greatest of God's Old Testament saints had been unable to bear, was borne by the God-man, the Lord Jesus Christ, and he did it as our substitute; he did it for us. By remembering the law we begin to grasp what Jesus had to do to achieve our salvation.

32

THE LAST WORD

'See, I will send you the prophet Elijah before that great and dreadful day of the LORD comes. He will turn the hearts of the fathers to their children, and the hearts of the children to their fathers; or else I will come and strike the land with a curse' (Malachi 4:5-6).

It cannot go unnoticed that the Old Testament ends with the word 'curse'. I think we could make too much of this, as if it alone embodied the expectation of the Mosaic law, or that it intended to cast a shadow over Malachi's hope. But it does seem to put in bold relief the contrast between the law and the gospel to come. Because Malachi's theme is *You are loved*, any warning that God gives through him flows from his love. Why else would he bother to warn his people? His warning is motivated by love. *'The Lord disciplines those he loves, and he punishes everyone he accepts as a son'* (Heb. 12:6).

These final words are a pronouncement, a declaration. They almost certainly refer back to, *'"See, I will send my messenger, who will prepare the way before me. Then suddenly the Lord you are seeking will come to his temple; the messenger of the covenant, whom you desire, will come," says the Lord Almighty'* (3:1). When the prophet refers to Elijah in the verse we are looking at, it most likely refers to him as 'the messenger'. But it will also be recalled that the name Malachi means messenger.

God's pronouncement is also a prophecy. It is a surprising word. Who would have expected God's message of love to end with a curse, or the Old Testament to close with the word. How is the curse fulfilled, and what has it to do with the messenger? It seems to say that if Elijah does not bring parents and children together God will curse the land. It is, therefore, a prophecy that gives hope to dysfunctional families because it implies family unity. The verse, however, leaves us with a problem. How are we to understand its fulfilment? It most certainly refers to John the Baptist because Gabriel quotes it when speaking to Zechariah. *'And he (John the Baptist) will go on before the Lord, in the spirit and power of Elijah, to turn the hearts of the fathers to their children and the disobedient to the wisdom of the righteous – to make ready a people prepared for the Lord'* (Luke 1:17). So Malachi is not referring to Elijah himself, but to the one who would go *'in the spirit and power of Elijah'.* On the other hand, Jesus says that *'John. ... He is the Elijah who was to come'* (Matt. 11:14).

But that is not the only question these verses raise. What does Malachi mean by Elijah coming before the great and dreadful day of the Lord? This language hints at Jesus' second coming rather than his coming as a baby. And I am not sure that there is much evidence that John the Baptist's ministry resulted in the reunion of fathers and children. It makes me wonder whether these verses have a dual fulfilment, that they refer in part to our Lord's first coming, and in part to his second coming.

We know that Elijah was very popular in Malachi's day and that the Jews looked forward to his reappearing. He was mentioned in grace after meals. 'May God in his mercy send us the prophet Elijah', was the form of words used. Elijah's name also appeared in the circumcision ceremony. And during the Passover meal a cup of wine was poured for him. When grace was said at the Passover, a child opened the door in expectation of Elijah's coming. And after Jesus' coming, we have Elijah's appearance when the Lord was transfigured on the mountain-top.

Is it possible, then, that we are not yet finished with Elijah yet? I don't say that because he did not die, rather was taken to heaven in a whirlwind, though some assert that he must at some time die because Scripture says that all men must die. But that limits God; he may have chosen that some should not see death. While I raise the question about a possible future role for Elijah, I don't provide an answer. I simply leave the door open to the possibility, and Malachi's final words do not discourage me from doing that.

Scripture gives us no evidence that the ministry of John the Baptist made a big impact on family life, even through Gabriel made that promise. However, we have every right to assume that did happen because we are convinced of God's truthfulness in his word. The reference to the great and dreadful day of the Lord tends towards an eschatological fulfilment, and it gives us hope in these perilous times that families will be reunited. Never has such a need been so obvious. Dysfunctional families, where parents and children don't communicate, is the most common malady I can think of.

Malachi certainly points to a prophetic wake-up call to families. God cares about families. The nuclear family was his idea. The most important institution on the planet is not the government, nor it is an educational system, nor even the church, it is the family. Focus on the family is the need of the day. We should all pray that God will soon move in the hearts of fathers, making them care about their families. The hearts of children would respond. Fathers' hearts would be turned first, then their children. Were this to take place on a large scale in our day it would be the equivalent of any miracle seen in the ministry of Elijah himself.

The hearts of many of us who are fathers are on our jobs, our careers, financial security and personal happiness. They should be on our children. Nobody has ever said on his deathbed that he wished he had spent more time in the office, but there must have been many who said they wished they had spent more time with their families. Fathers' hearts focussing on their families would do more to change society than anything else I can think of. While only God can make that happen, a prophetic wake-up call would reveal our priorities and move us to make major changes in our family lives.

God says that if this restoration of the family does not happen he will strike the land with a curse, because if the family is not healed there will be no hope for the nation. The only outcome would be God's judgment. It is fitting, therefore, that Malachi ends his prophecy in this way, remembering that it was delivered to a people who had disregarded their families and brought God's displeasure. We can, however, trace the rainbow through the rain and nourish the hope that a better day is coming for families. And those who rely on Christ's finished work have the sure and certain hope that a better day is coming, the best day of all, because Malachi's message applies to all his people. He says to each one of us, 'You are loved.'

OTHER BOOKS
BY
R. T. KENDALL

R.T. KENDALL

*A Man After
God's Own Heart*

GOD'S RELATIONSHIP WITH DAVID AND WITH YOU

A Man After God's Own Heart

God's relationship with David – and with you

R.T. Kendall

Twice God says that in King David he has found 'a man after my own heart (Ist Samuel 13:14, Acts 13:22). God was personally involved with David, there was something about him which he really liked.

David was a sensitive man, a man with deep feelings, he was a poet and musician but he was also Israel's greatest King and one of the greatest ever military leaders. But these things seem to matter less to God than the soul of the man.

David wrote 'the Lord confides in those who fear him' (Psalm 25:14), it is a great honour to have someone confide in you – but to think that God would confide in a human being is amazing! David was someone with whom God chose to share his heart.

If you wish to know what it is like to be confided in by God – to become a man after God's own heart too – then this book will help you discover what such a relationship is like.

ISBN 1 85792 382 0

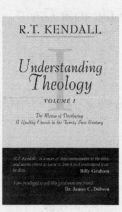

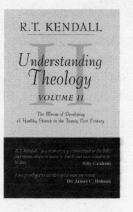

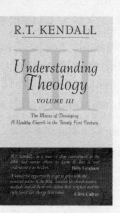

Understanding Theology
Volumes I, II & III

*The Means of Developing a Healthy Church
in the Twenty First Century*

R.T. Kendall

*R T Kendall....is a man of deep commitment to the Bible and
wants others to know it, love it and understand it as he does.*
Billy Graham

*A wonderful opportunity to get to grips with the essential truths of
the Bible. Suitable for church leaders, students and all those who
believe that scripture and the Holy Spirit can change lives today.*
Clive Calver

These volumes of Understanding Theology have been
tremendously well received. They have almost created a new
genre due to their unique means of communicating truths from
the Bible. Taken from subjects covered in the Westminster School
of Theology they are a comprehensive handbook of practical
theology.

The content and format of the books are their strength – each
volume contains a list of doctrinal subjects that occur again
and again in adult Sunday Schools, House Groups, Bible studies
and congregational meetings. Each subject is dealt with in outline
form – giving you the maximum information in a way that is
easily digestible.

If you want to work your way through a doctrine and its practical
outcome then Understanding Theology has been designed for
you.

Volume 1 ISBN 1 85792 429 0
Volume 2 ISBN 1 85792 537 8
Volume 3 ISBN 1 85792 5815

HIGHER GROUND

Insights from the Psalms of Ascent

RT Kendall

Which way is your Christian Life going?

Every year the Jewish pilgrims would go to Jerusalem to keep the annual feasts. On the way, to help focus their thoughts, they would especially sing psalms 120-134, commonly called the Psalms of Ascent.

Just as God used these psalms to guide his people on their way to the temple so today he can use these same psalms to effect a change in his church, to bring people into a closer relationship with him and produce a radical change in lifestyle on our journey to Heaven.

RT Kendall doesn't give us a line by line commentary but instead takes each psalm's theme and shows how our lives should be different from the world's when we are moving together to Higher Ground

ISBN 1 85792 158 5

CHRISTIAN FOCUS PUBLICATIONS

We publish books for all ages.

STAYING FAITHFUL

In dependence upon God we seek to help make his infallible word, the Bible, relevant. Our aim is to ensure that the Lord Jesus Christ is presented as the only hope to obtain forgiveness of sin, live a useful life, and look forward to heaven with him.

REACHING OUT

Christ's last command requires us to reach out to our world with his gospel. We seek to help fulfil that by publishing books that point people towards Jesus and for them to develop a Christ-like maturity. We aim to equip all levels of readers for life, work, ministry and mission.

Books in our adult range are published in three imprints:-
Christian Focus contains popular works including biographies, commentaries, basic doctrine, and Christian living. Our children's books are also published in this imprint.
Christian Heritage contains classic writings from the past.
Mentor focuses on books written at a level suitable for Bible College and seminary students, pastors, and other serious readers; the imprint includes commentaries, doctrinal studies, examination of current issues, and church history.

Christian Focus Publications, Ltd
Geanies House, Fearn, Ross-shire,
IV20 ITW, Scotland, United Kingdom
info@christianfocus.com

www.christianfocus.com